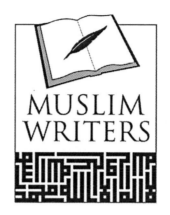

MUSLIM
WRITERS

ALSO BY LINDA D. DELGADO

ISLAMIC ROSE BOOKS SERIES

The Visitors (Book One)

Hijab-Ez Friends (Book Two)

Stories (Book Three)

Saying Goodbye (Book Four)

NON-FICTION

A Muslim's Guide to Publishing and Marketing

Halal Food, Fun and Laughter

Linda D. Delgado

Muslim Writers Publishing
Tempe, Arizona

Muslim Writers Publishing
P.O. Box 27362
Tempe, Arizona 85285
USA

Publisher's website at www.MuslimWritersPublishing.com

Library of Congress Catalog Number 2005935844

ISBN 0-9767861-5-x
ISBN 978-0-9767861-5-3

Illustrations by: Shirley Gavin
Cover design by: Zoltan Rac-Sabo
Book design by: Leila Joiner

Printed in the USA

Halal Food,
Fun
and
Laughter

Thanks!

I offer my thanks and my appreciation to the many sister-friends around the world who so generously gave me their original recipes, funny food stories and funny food poems to help create this book for the pleasure of Allah, and those who will enjoy the recipes and odd humor contained in the pages of this cookbook.

Some of my contributors wished to remain anonymous. Other sister-friends agreed to the inclusion of their names as contributors:. Corey Habbas, Saaleha Bhamjee, Judy Nelson Eldawy, Shima Hashim, Nur Sazlina, Karen Nooruddin, Pamela K. Taylor, Juli Herman, Fatimah Asmal, Nadia Hamed, Nicole Bovey Alhakawati, and Nancy Biddle. May Allah reward all of you for your generosity.

Special thanks to Saira (AKA) Linda Kingston, thank you so much for lending me your many wonderful original recipes from your family. Without your help I would not have been able to provide so many unusual, creative, and fantastic halal recipes which make this cookbook so unique.

Special Thanks

Most cookbooks are filled with pictures of wonderful meals that are supposed to represent the recipes included in the cookbooks. Now, whenever I tried out a new recipe, I would look at my final result and many times it just didn't look quite like the picture! Did I do something wrong? Rather than have my "cooks" wonder like I do, if the pictures really show what the finished dish looks like, I decided to create a bit of humor to replace the usual pictures you would expect to see in a cookbook. A special thank you to my friend and illustrator, Shirley Gavin for the humorous illustrations. A very special thanks for Ms. Don't Do. Special Thanks to Zoltan Rac-Sabo for creating the Mr. Cake Slice illustration for the cookbook's cover.

Last but not least is my thanks to my copyeditor Molly Brewsaugh for her fine editing work and Marie Rieuwers for her expert cookbook content editing and advice.

NOTE: I have kept each recipe as close to how it was given to me. This will account for the different styles, measurement and temperature scales, and terminology found in the cookbook's recipes.

Table of Contents

SPECIALTIES

Introduction

Now, I have never been a gourmet cook, but I have always been a gourmet eater! In the Spring of 2002 I began gathering recipes from my sister-friends from around the world. Their recipes and a few of my own are offered for your dining pleasure.

I selected five main categories for placing the recipes in a more or less logical grouping. Placement in each category was at random. I haven't any preference for one recipe over another as I love each of them! The short-short stories, poems, Qur'an and Hadith verses were also placed at random, but with a purpose. They are included in the cookbook as "little jewels" among the treasure of recipes.

This cookbook combines a winning "recipe" for a healthy life-style: good food, some fun and laughter and last but most importantly, remembrances of Allah, by adding some wonderful Qur'an and Hadith to the mix to help create a happier and healthier recipe for your life. My favorite of many favorite Qur'an verses:

"For without doubt
In the remembrance of Allah
do hearts find satisfaction.
For those who believe and work righteousness,
Is every blessedness,
And a beautiful place of (final) return."

Surah Ar-Ra'ad 13: 28 - 29

Allah willing, you will enjoy this special cookbook and I would love to hear from you so be sure to write to me via email at:

publisher@ MuslimWritersPublishing.com.

What is Halal?

Glad you asked! As Muslims, we live in submission to Allah (SWT). We live and die by the guidelines He gave us for how and when to pray, how to dress and how to conduct our daily lives. Among these daily standards are very specific rules which we follow concerning what we may or may not eat and drink and how the meat we consume should be slaughtered. Here are the basics.

Muslims may not take in alcohol of any kind (not even if it is "cooked off" in the process). This applies to cooking with cooking wine, sherry, or even the use of vanilla or almond or other "extracts" soaked in vodka.

We may not eat any part of the pig. This includes the use of gelatin derived from the hooves of the pig as well—only beef or fish gelatin is considered halal.

Muslims may not consume the flesh of carnivorous animals. The exception to this is that anything which comes from the sea is permissible. Fish, beef, lamb, goat and chicken are the mainstays of the Muslim's diet, but there are guidelines as to how these animals should be treated up to and during their slaughter. What makes meat halal are two things: 1. the animal is permissible to eat (e.g. cow, goat, rabbit, sheep, etc.) and 2. the animal is slaughtered in a prescribed way, which is that the throat is cut, in the name of Allah, and the blood is immediately drained from the body.

Just as the world has learned the definition of kosher, the world is now also learning the term halal. Many grocery stores now carry products with the label halal on frozen meats and pizzas. "Jello" and marshmallows are available with halal gelatin as the main ingredient. Much research goes into questioning the makers of candies and processed food goods to establish which are halal and which are not. If you want more information on this topic, search out Understanding Islam at www.understadingislam.com.

Special thanks to Noura Shamma for doing the research required to provide an explanation for the word Halal.

Handy Measurement Conversions

How to Convert Temperature Measurements

Several different temperature scales exist—the Celsius scale sets freezing and boiling points of water at 0 and 100, respectively, while the Fahrenheit scale sets them at 32 and 212. Here's how to convert between the two types.

Multiply the Celsius temperature reading by 9/5, and then add 32 to get the temperature in Fahrenheit: (9/5 * C) + 32 = F.

Subtract 32 from the Fahrenheit temperature, and then multiply this quantity by 5/9 to get the temperature in Celsius: (F - 32) * 5/9 = C.

An easier way to remember temperature conversions is to use estimates, such as 2 for 9/5. For example, multiply temperature in Celsius by 2, and then add 32 to get the approximate temperature in Fahrenheit.

Convert Measurements Between U.S. and Metric Systems

One ounce equals about 28 grams (28.350 g).
1 gram equals 0.035 ounce
Sixteen ounces equal 1 pound.
One pound equals 0.45 kilograms.
1 kilogram equals 2.2 pounds

Liquid Measurements

Three tsps. equal 1 tbsp.
Sixteen tbsp. equal 1 cup
Eight fluid ounces equal 1 cup
Two cups equal 1 pint
Two pints equal 1 quart.
Four quarts equal 1 gallon

Convert Between U.S. and Metric Systems

One tsp. equals about 5 milliliters.
One tbsp. equals about 15 milliliters.
One fluid ounce equals about 30 milliliters (29.573 ml)
One cup equals about 240 milliliters (236.584 ml).
One quart equals about 1 liter (0.94635 L)
One gallon equals about 4 liters (3.7854 L)

I'm A Dunker And I'm Not Ashamed Of It!

—Fatima Asmal—

I am a lover of tea, and confess to being a shameless 'dunker'—rusks, buttered toast, chocolaty biscuits, you name it, I dunk it! It definitely runs in my family. (My brother's midnight snack often consists of two cups of tea-one for dunking and one for drinking, because by the time he's done with dunking the first cup is empty!)

I recently attended a function, and when tea was served, together with a platter of yummy looking biscuits, I cast an apologetic glance at my neighbor and explained that I had to do what I was about to do. I was pleased to hear that I am definitely not alone!

"Don't worry," she laughed. "Before I met my husband, I thought it was a disgusting habit, then we got married, and I picked it up from him, as did my little daughter. One day we went to a function, and she was walking with me, a biscuit in her hand, when she saw a very distinguished and stern-looking foreign Shaykh (Islamic scholar) seated at a table drinking a glass filled with soft-drink. Well, my daughter marches up to him, and in one movement, dunks her biscuit into his soft-drink, and eats it. This man was horrified. I just walked the other way. I didn't want him to know I was her mum!

Soups and Salads

Samosas Calcutta Style

Ingredients:

COVER:
2 cups plain flour
3 tbsp. melted ghee
Salt to taste

FILLING:
1 cup cauliflower
2 cups potatoes boiled
6-7 green chilies
1 tsp. ginger grated
1 tsp. panchphoran
½ tbsp. coriander finely chopped
½ tsp. amchoor (dried mango) powder
½ tsp. garam masala
¼ tsp. turmeric
Salt to taste
½ tbsp. raisins
1 tbsp. cashew pieces
3-4 pinches asafoetida
1 tbsp. oil
Oil for deep-frying

Method:

Sift flour and salt together. Add ghee and mix well.

Add water to knead a soft dough.

Cover with moist cloth and keep aside for 30 minutes.

Brush liberally with ghee, knead, cover again and keep aside.

Filling:

Grate cauliflower, mash potatoes and finely chop green chilies.

Heat oil, add cashews and fry till light golden.

Add panchphoran and allow to splutter, add cauliflower.

Add all other ingredients and mix well.

Take off fire. Keep aside.

Method:

Make small balls, the size of small lemons from dough. Knead one into thin chappati about 5" diameter.

Cut into half, take one, fold into cone, seal edge with some water.

Fill with one tbsp. filling, seal open edges to form triangular pyramid.

Seal edges and corners well with moist fingers.

Make four or five, deep-fry in hot oil till golden and crisp.

Repeat for all filling and dough.

Serve hot with green and tamarind chutneys

MAKING TIME: 1 hour

MAKES: 20 approximately

Judy's Egyptian Salads and Dressings

Salads:

In the Middle East, salads are made using tomatoes, cucumber, onion, carrots (thinly diced) fresh herbs, (including mint sometimes), and seasoned with salt, pepper and a bit of vinegar. This is quite nice when eaten on top of rice and Camelia likes it when I mix the salad and rice together into one dish. Conspicuously absent is lettuce—which they do have but eat all by its lonesome.

Dressings:

My sister-in-law blends her own seasoning mix. Into one jar, she adds salt, black pepper, red pepper, coriander (called kusbarrah) and cumin. I make one with salt, cumin (a small amount goes a long way), some garlic powder and black pepper. Depending on the amounts you mix it in, the taste will change. Experiment and see what works for you— just work in small amounts till you have an idea of what you want.

Judy's Change-of-Pace Quick Ideas

Quick Recipes:

Hard boil a couple eggs and fry them whole in a bit of oil, sprinkle with salt or the seasoning mixture of your choice and eat. Not for everyday as far as I am concerned but it makes a change of pace.

If I am frying anything, I like to slice up some green peppers and onions, fry them till brown and soft, drain well, sprinkle with seasoning, wrap in bread and eat.

American Style Mac and Cheese

Ingredients:

1 medium size package of macaroni (8 oz.)
½ cup of margarine
4-6 tbsp. flour
4 cups of milk
½ lb. sharp or natural-mild longhorn style cheese, grated
½ lb. Cheddar cheese, grated
Salt and black pepper, to taste

Method:

Cook the macaroni until almost done, cool in cold water while preparing the cheese sauce.

In a large saucepan melt the margarine or butter on a low heat. When melted, add the flour and mix until a paste forms. Next add the 4 cups of milk and stir until the milk is warm. Add the grated cheese and continue stirring until all the cheese is melted. You should have a creamy cheese sauce. Be sure to watch closely and stir a lot to avoid sticking or burning of the sauce.

Next spread margarine on the sides and bottom of a glass baking dish. Drain the cooled macaroni and pour into the baking dish. Now add the cheese sauce to the macaroni and stir until the macaroni is fully covered.

Bake at 325° until a brown crust begins to form on the edges of the macaroni.

Serve with ground black pepper and a green salad.

The Prophet used to pray after taking his food: "All praise be to Allah who fed us and gave us drink and made us Muslims." (Tirmidhi Hadith)

Grilled Chicken and Walnut Salad—USA

This wonderful lunch treat is great on toasted rye
or served on a lush bed of lettuce!

Ingredients:

3 boneless, skinless grilled
chicken breasts (chopped and
shredded) or (2) 5 oz. cans of
breast of chicken)
½ cup fat free mayonnaise
1 tbsp. Dijon or Creole
mustard
1/3 cup halved seedless red
grapes
½ cup chopped walnuts
2 tbsp. Cajun spice or one
each of salt and pepper
½ stalk finely chopped celery
(optional)

Method:

1. First, chop and shred the
chicken breasts leaving some
chunky pieces or place the
canned chicken into a large
bowl.

2. Combine chicken, mayo,
Dijon mustard and mix until
chicken is fully coated and
consistency is even.

3. Add spice, celery, walnuts
and grapes and stir in evenly.

4. Serve on a sandwich or bed
of lettuce and enjoy!

VARIATION: you could also
add chopped red pepper for
extra flavor!

Chickpea Delight

Ingredients:

1 quart water
1 cup uncooked chickpeas
2 onions, finely chopped
1 tsp. ground turmeric
2 tsp. ground ginger
1 tsp. ground black pepper;
salt (to taste)
1 tsp. ground cinnamon
½ lb. beef, preferably
diced fillet
¼ bunch cilantro
½ bunch flat leaf parsley
¼ bunch chopped lovage,
optional
10 vine tomatoes, peeled
and seeded, grated or
chopped finely
½ cup rice or crushed
vermicelli
1 cup water-flour mixture
(1 tbsp. flour dissolved in
1 cup water)
1 cup fava beans, soaked and
drained
1 cup lentils (optional)
2 tbsp. olive oil

Method:

Place the following into a
deep saucepan and cover with
water: chickpeas, chopped
onion, spices, meat.

Bring these ingredients to a
boil and simmer until the
chickpeas are tender.

Chop the cilantro, flat leaf
parsley, and lovage, if used,
and grind in pestle and
mortar to release the flavors.

Then, add the herbs, pulped
tomatoes, and rice.

After about 5 minutes, add
the water/flour mixture. This
helps the soup thicken and
lighten in color.

Finally add the fava beans,
and lentils. Simmer for about
20 to 30 minutes

Season, with salt, to taste.
Drizzle with olive oil and
serve with bread and sweet
dates.

Grilled-Eggplant Salad-Cilantro-Chile Dressing

Ingredients:

DRESSING:
¼ cup fresh lime juice
2 tbsp. chopped fresh cilantro
1 tbsp. brown sugar
1 tbsp. Thai fish sauce
1 tbsp. minced seeded Thai, hot red, or Serrano chile
2 garlic cloves, minced

SALAD:
12 cherry tomatoes, quartered
12 (1/2-inch-thick) slices eggplant (about 2 lbs.)
¼ tsp. salt, divided
cooking spray
6 (1/2-inch-thick) slices red onion
¼ cup torn mint leaves
¼ cup torn basil leaves

Method:

To prepare dressing, combine first 6 ingredients in a bowl; stir well with a whisk. Prepare grill or broiler.

To prepare salad, combine tomatoes and dressing, and set aside.

Sprinkle eggplant with 1/8 tsp. salt.

Place eggplant on a grill rack or broiler pan coated with cooking spray; cook 5 minutes on each side or until eggplant is done.

Remove eggplant from grill rack or pan; set aside.

Sprinkle onion with 1/8 tsp. salt. Place onion on grill rack or broiler pan coated with cooking spray; cook for 5 minutes on each side or until onion is tender.

Arrange eggplant and onion slices on 6 plates.

Top with tomato mixture; sprinkle with mint and basil.

Shima's GADO-GADO
Malay Salad with Peanut Gravy

Ingredients:

GRAVY:
2.5 tbsp. of crunchy peanut
butter (you may use blended
roasted groundnuts)
3 tbsp. vegetable oil (ghee is
better; made up of buttermilk)
2 medium sized onions.
4 cloves garlic.
1 tbsp. tomato puree/paste
chili powder or fresh chilies
to taste
ginger root about 1.5 cm.
lemon grass (optional, but it
really does make a difference
if you use it)
3-4 tbsp. coconut milk (As an
alternative, you may use milk.
For the health conscious, you
may omit both types of milk.)
sugar (to taste)
some vegetable or any other
stock

Method:

Blend onion, garlic, ginger,
and fresh chilies into a paste.
If you don't wish to do that,
you may chop them all up
finely. Crush lemon grass.
Heat oil in pan or pot. Add in
the crushed lemon grass,
followed by the blended paste.
Sauté till you feel the paste is
rather cooked. Add in tomato
paste. Stir for another 2-3
min. Add peanut butter together with stock. The consistency or thickness of the sauce
should be similar to making
tomato based pasta sauces.
The amount of stock you will
need to add will vary. Add salt
and sugar to taste. Leave to
boil for 5-6 min, but stir the
mixture once in a while to
avoid burning the peanut
sauce.

Feel free to add more peanut
butter if you feel that the
gravy's not nutty enough.
Once done, the sauce will look
like a bolognaise sauce in
color but brownish, and the

oil will 'ooze' out if you leave it alone for a while.

With this gravy, we normally eat a salad made up of vegetables which are boiled. For example: potatoes, cabbage, bean sprouts, or green beans. We then add cucumber and fried bean curd. All this we toss together with the Malay traditional 'rice cake', which I make in the 'modern way', by cooking the rice till it's rather soft so that it's easy to mash. After mashing the rice, I store it in a bowl or any container. Cover the rice and place a heavy object on it because this will keep the rice really, really compact. Put it aside and when it's cool, you just need to cut it up into cubes. Add it together with the rest of the vegetables, crush some prawn/fish crackers, and then pour the gravy over the dish. Simply delicious!

Our Lord! Pour out on us patience and constancy, and make us die as those who have surrendered themselves unto You. (7:126)

Taste-of-Summer Spaghetti Sauce—Italy

Ingredients:

6-8 large, ripe tomatoes—
if you can take them out of
your own garden, so much
the better! You want to end up
with about 6 cups of chopped
tomatoes.
½ cup fresh basil leaves, torn
into small pieces
2 cloves garlic, crushed
1/3 cup Extra Virgin Olive Oil
Salt and fresh-ground black
pepper, to taste

Method:

Chop the tomatoes (don't
bother to peel) and put them
into a clear glass jar.

Add the other ingredients and
stir well.

Put the jar (put a lid on it!)
outside in a sunny location
and let it "cook" in the sun,
like sun-tea. Don't worry, it's
not going to "spoil."

Serve it sun-warmed (don't
heat it) over cooked spaghetti
noodles, topped with Parmesan Cheese.

SERVINGS: Makes enough
sauce for 1 lb. of pasta

Love Food

—Nadia Hamed—

I love to cook. I love to make food.
A good soup or salad can set the mood.
I love taste, texture and smell.
I love herbs and spices as well.
I love to hear people say, "Great!!!".
And take another helping before it's too late.
I love the laughter and smiles all around.
And through our food we're bound.
I love the time it really took to make this meal.
And all the stomachs it may fill.

Potato Salad for Children—USA

Ingredients:

3 white Idaho style potatoes,
boiled in their skins until
cooked but firm
3 large eggs, hardboiled
1 medium can whole pitted
black olives
Miracle Whip Light Salad
Dressing; quantity needed
to cover potato/egg/olive
mixture
1 tbsp. yellow mustard

Method:

Boil potatoes, but do not peel
them until after they are
cooked and cooled to at least
room temperature. They will
be easier to dice if you place
them in the refrigerator for an
hour or two. Boil eggs and
peel them after they have
cooled to room temperature.
Mix the diced potatoes, eggs
and olives in a bowl. Add salt
to taste. Add Miracle Whip
Salad Dressing to the mixture.
The eggs, potatoes and olives
should be covered. Finally,
add the mustard to give the
salad some color. Chill before
serving.

Servings:

NOTE: Add one potato and
one egg for each additional
serving.

SECRET: Be sure to use
the salad dressing and not
mayonnaise. Most kids don't
like mayonnaise but like the
salad dressing. They also like
to poke their fingers into the
whole, pitted olives.

Adult Version:

Add ½ diced onion, ½ cup
chopped celery, parsley, 1
tbsp. Cumin, and black pepper to taste.

The Holy Qur'an 2:172—O ye who believe! Eat of the
good things that We have provided for you, and be
grateful to Allah, if it is Him ye worship.

Coconut Bondas

Ingredients:

1 cup coconut, grated
5 potatoes, boiled and mashed
6 green chilies, chopped
1 tsp. cumin seeds
1 tsp. mustard seeds
3 bread slices
3 tbsp. coriander leaves, chopped
A few raisins
A few chopped cashew nuts
Salt to taste
Oil for deep frying
2 tbsp. oil, for sautéing coconut
1 egg, beaten

Method:

Heat 2 tbsp. oil in a pan
Fry mustard seeds and cumin seeds, till they splutter.

Add green chilies, coconut, salt, raisins and cashew nuts.

Fry for 5 min.
Let the mixture cool.

Dry grind the bread slices.
Add to the mashed potatoes, salt and bread powder.

Mix well to soft dough.
Take a small portion of potato dough, flatten on your palm, fill with coconut stuffing and shape into a small ball.

Repeat with the rest of the dough and stuffing.

Roll in beaten egg and deep fry in hot oil till golden brown.

Serve with green chutney and tamarind chutney.

Rice Porridge

It's so simple, you won't fail with this one!

1. Boil a handful of rice and some chicken (fish or any seafood is good also) in about 3 cups of water or stock together with some chopped veggies: carrots, potatoes, peppers, radish, mushrooms, pumpkins, just use your imagination!

Add in about an inch of bruised ginger (optional). Personally, I like to add in some ground nuts/lentils as well. This gives it a unique flavor. Add in some chopped fresh coriander and leave it to simmer for about ½ hour on a low fire.

Stir occasionally so that the rice will not burn at bottom. You may occasionally add more water to make the porridge consistency that suits your taste.

2. Once it becomes porridge, add in some milk or better still coconut milk if you have any. Let it boil for another 5 minutes or so.

3. Sauté some chopped garlic in olive oil and add to the porridge. OR, you may just boil the chopped garlic together with the porridge beforehand.

4. Ready to serve with chopped spring onions, pepper or an omelet that has been cut into strips or just plain old parsley.

Walah! Happy Cooking!

Rose Petal Tomato—Italy

Ingredients:

fresh cilantro (coriander)
1 Roma tomato
feta cheese
basil
black seeds
2 tbsp. olive oil

Method:

Place fresh cilantro in a "wreath" type arrangement on the plate.

Take the "Roma" tomato (better taste than your regular tomato) and cut out the stem section.

Turn it upside-down so that it is standing on the end that you cut.

Slice, starting from the outside, little "rose petals" (just slice straight down, but don't cut all the way through - like you would a radish.

Turn the tomato and keep making petals.

When you have finished cutting the "petals," put it on top of the cilantro in the center of the wreath.

Crumble some Feta cheese around the wreath, then sprinkled basil and black seeds on it.

Last step—I drizzle about 2 tbsp of olive oil all over it.

Chinese Slaw

This slaw tastes great with grilled teriyaki chicken or beef.

Ingredients:

4 cups shredded green cabbage
¾ cup diagonally sliced green onions
½ cup shredded carrot
½ cup thinly sliced red bell pepper
2 tbsp. low-sodium tamari or soy sauce
1 tbsp. sesame seeds, toasted
1 tbsp. grated peeled fresh ginger
1 tbsp. mirin (substitute rice water)
1 tbsp. rice vinegar
1½ tsp. dark sesame oil
2 tsp. sugar

Method:

Combine all ingredients in a large bowl. Let stand at least 15 minutes.

The Holy Qur'an 6:99—It is He Who sendeth down rain from the skies: with it We produce vegetation of all kinds: from some We produce green (crops), out of which We produce grain, heaped up (at harvest); out of the date-palm and its sheaths (or spathes) (come) clusters of dates hanging low and near: and (then there are) gardens of grapes, and olives, and pomegranates, each similar (in kind) yet different (in variety): when they begin to bear fruit, feast your eyes with the fruit and the ripeness thereof. Behold! In these things there are signs for people who believe.

Lemon-Basil Bean Bowl

Ingredients:

1/3 cup chopped fresh basil
1 tsp. grated lemon rind
2 tbsp. fresh lemon juice
1 tbsp. olive oil
2½ tsp. Dijon mustard
½ tsp. sugar
¼ tsp. salt
¼ tsp. freshly ground black pepper
1 garlic clove, minced
4 cups (1-inch) cut green beans (about 1 lb.)
1½ cups chopped plum tomato
1 (10-ounce) package frozen baby lima beans, cooked and drained
4 low-fat turkey bacon slices, cooked and crumbled (drained)

Method:

Combine first 9 ingredients in a bowl; stir with a whisk.

Steam the green beans, covered, for 8 minutes or until tender. Combine green beans, tomato, and lima beans in a large bowl. Pour basil mixture over bean mixture, and toss well. Sprinkle with turkey bacon.

Eastern Vegetable Pot

Ingredients:

¾ cup long grain white rice
1 cup fresh sliced mushrooms
½ cup chopped green bell pepper
½ cup chopped red bell pepper
1 cup salted cashew pieces
1 cup chopped green onions
½ kg fresh bean sprouts
2½ kg fresh spinach
3 stalks celery, chopped
½ cup vegetable oil
¼ cup soy sauce
1 tsp. chopped fresh parsley
½ tsp. crushed garlic

Method:

In a saucepan bring 1½ cups salted water to a boil.

Add ¾ cup rice, reduce heat, cover and simmer for 20 minutes.

Drain any excess water. Refrigerate rice until chilled.

Combine the chilled cooked rice, mushrooms, green peppers, red peppers, cashews, green onions, bean sprouts, spinach and celery in a large bowl.

Blend the vegetable oil, soy sauce, parsley and crushed garlic in a separate bowl.

Pour the dressing over the salad 1 hour before serving and toss well

Uruguayan Bean Salad

Ingredients:

3 cups canned fava or kidney
beans, drained and rinsed
1 cup chopped seeded tomato
¾ cup finely chopped onion
¼ cup chopped fresh flat-leaf
parsley
3 tbsp. red vinegar
2 tbsp. extra-virgin olive oil
1 tsp. dried oregano
½ tsp. crushed red pepper
(dry or flakes)
½ tsp. freshly ground black
pepper
¼ tsp. salt

Method:

Combine all the ingredients in
a bowl, and toss gently.

Umm

—Nadia Hamed—

The smell drifted out the door,
near the ceiling, near the floor.

Over the bushes into the street,
"Umm, what is it that smells so neat!!"

I hear a knock and put down my spoon.
I open the door and what do I see?
All my neighbors gathered 'round me.

"What's that smell? Can we come in?"
"Yes, of course, it's nice to see you all again!"

Main Dishes

Nur's Peanut Chicken Breast

Ingredients:

¼ cup peanut butter
2 tbsp. chopped, salted peanuts
2 tbsp. soy sauce
1 tbsp. minced onions
1 tbsp. minced parsley
1 clove garlic—crushed
Several drops of red pepper sauce
1/8 tsp. ground ginger
4 whole chicken breasts—skinned and boned
2 tbsp. soy sauce
2 tbsp. honey
1 tbsp. melted butter
10½ ounces of chicken stock
1 tbsp. cornstarch

Method:

Mix peanut butter, peanuts, 2 tbsp. soy sauce, onion, parsley, garlic, pepper sauce, and ginger.

Spread on inside of each chicken breast. Fold in half; close with small skewer or a toothpick. Place in slow-cooking pot. Mix remaining 2 tbsp. soy sauce with honey, butter, and broth; pour over chicken. Cover and cook on low for 4 to 5 hours. Remove chicken from pot. Turn control to high. Dissolve cornstarch in small amount of cold water; stir into sauce. Cook on high for about 15 minutes. Spoon sauce on chicken and serve

None of you should regard any act of goodwill as too insignificant. Should you have nothing with you to offer a brother in need, at least greet him with goodly cheer, and add water to the gravy that you prepare for your food to increase its quantity and share it with a neighbor in need. (Tirmidhi Hadith.)

Seafood Paella—Spain

Ingredients:

BROTH:
3 cups water
1 cup dry white grape juice
1 tsp. saffron threads
2 (8-ounce) bottles clam juice

HERB BLEND:
1 cup chopped fresh parsley
1/3 cup fresh lemon juice
1 tbsp. olive oil
1 tsp. dried tarragon
2 large garlic cloves, minced

PAELLA:
1 lb. monkfish or other firm
white fish fillets
16 unpeeled jumbo shrimp
(about 1 lb.)
1 tbsp. olive oil
2 cups finely chopped onion
1 cup finely chopped red bell
pepper
1 cup canned diced tomatoes,
undrained
1 tsp. sweet paprika
½ tsp. crushed red pepper
3 garlic cloves, minced
3 cups uncooked Arborio rice
or other short-grain rice
1 cup frozen green peas
16 little neck clams

1 (7-ounce) jar sliced
pimento, drained
2 tbsp. fresh lemon juice

Method:

To prepare broth, combine
the first 4 ingredients in a
saucepan. Bring to a simmer.
(Do not boil).

Keep warm over low heat.

To prepare herb blend,
combine parsley and next 4
ingredients (parsley through 2
garlic cloves); set aside.

To prepare paella, trim
connective tissue from monkfish; cut into 1-inch pieces.

Peel and devein shrimp,
leaving tails attached..

Heat 1 tbsp. oil in a large
paella pan or large skillet over
medium-high heat.

Add fish and shrimp; sauté 1
minute (the seafood mixture
will not be cooked through).
Remove seafood mixture
from pan, and keep warm.
Add onion and bell pepper to
pan, and sauté 5 minutes.

Add the tomatoes, paprika, crushed red pepper, and 3 garlic cloves; cook 5 minutes.

Add rice, and cook 1 minute, stirring constantly.

Stir in broth, herb blend, and peas.

Bring to a low boil, and cook 10 minutes, stirring frequently.

Add clams to pan, nestling them into rice mixture.

Cook 5 minutes or until shells open; discard any unopened shells.

Stir in the seafood mixture, and arrange shrimp, heads down, in rice mixture.

Arrange pimento slices spoke-like on top of rice mixture; cook 5 minutes.

Sprinkle with lemon juice. Remove from heat; cover with a towel and let stand 10 minutes.

Our Lord! You truly know all that we may hide [in our hearts] as well as all that we bring into the open, for nothing whatever, be it on earth or in heaven, remains hidden from Allah (14:38)

Food

—Saaleha Bhamjee—

Spicy koeksusters, freshly dipped
Thick cream, newly whipped
Biscuits a-baking in an oven warm
While outside rages a fierce summer storm
Childhood memories, tastes and smells
That ring familiar, comforting bells

The smell of braai in the summer air
Mielies dripping butter at the summer fair
Biltong drying in long rows
My hands sticky with roti dough
Childhood memories, tastes and smells
That ring familiar, comforting bells

Death by chocolate, chocolate cake
Milk tart, always Mum's greatest bake
Granny's khitchro, a filling broth
That is sure to result in a bit of sloth
Childhood memories, tastes and smells
That ring familiar, comforting bells

It's my turn now, with a brood of my own
It's up to me to set the tone
With red cakes a plenty, and fresh crunchies galore
Custard slice that has them asking for more
I must create the childhood memories, tastes and smells
That will always ring familiar, comforting bells

Bo Nuong Xa—Vietnamese

Marinated lemon grass beef skewers that can be
broiled or barbecued, a traditional Vietnamese dish,
best if dipped in Nuaoc Cham sauce.

Prep Time: 10 Minutes
Cook Time: 20 Minutes
Ready in: 4 Hrs, 30 Mins

Ingredients:

1½ lbs. sirloin tip, thinly sliced
2 tsp. white sugar
2 tbsp. soy sauce
1 tsp. ground black pepper
2 cloves garlic, minced
2 tsp. sesame seeds
2 lemon grass stalks, chopped
12 leaves romaine lettuce
3 tbsp. fresh cilantro, for garnish
6 leaves fresh basil
1 tbsp. chopped fresh mint leaves
2 green onions, thinly sliced

Method:

TO MARINATE: In a shallow nonporous dish or bowl combine the meat, sugar, soy sauce, pepper, garlic, lemon grass and sesame seeds. Mix together. Cover dish and refrigerate for 4 hours. During last hour, separately soak wooden skewers in water.

Preheat oven to broil OR lightly oil grill and preheat to high heat.

Remove meat and marinade from refrigerator. Thread meat onto pre-soaked skewers, accordion style. Broil or grill until done, about 15 to 20 minutes.

Serve hot from skewers or remove from skewers and place on lettuce leaves.

Garnish with cilantro, mint leaves, basil and sliced green onions and serve.

Saira's Panade (A French "Sopa Seca")

Ingredients:

½ loaf stale Ciabatta, French baguette, or other good-quality bread, sliced, and each slice cut in half
2-4 cups chicken meat (off the bone) in large pieces
2 tbsp. olive oil
4 cloves garlic, crushed
2 onions, thinly sliced
1 cup carrots, peeled and thinly sliced
1 tsp. thyme leaves
½ - 1 tsp. rosemary leaves (depending on how much you like rosemary)
2 cans chicken broth, plus enough water to make 4 cups OR 4 cups homemade broth
saffron, if desired
½ cup Parmesan cheese OR 1 cup grated Swiss cheese

Method:

Butter or oil a deep casserole (3 qt.) and set aside. Heat oven to 375° F.

Heat the olive oil in a skillet, and sauté the garlic, onion and carrots, along with the thyme and rosemary, until the onion is beginning to caramelize and the carrots are tender. Add salt and fresh ground black pepper to taste.

Layer in the casserole the bread, chicken, and vegetables, in that order, ending with a layer of bread.

If you are using saffron, pour the chicken broth into the skillet, bring it to a boil and add the saffron threads to steep, until the chicken broth is a nice yellow.

Ladle the broth over the layered ingredients in the casserole, and top with the cheese.

Bake the casserole for 30 to 40 minutes, or until the top is golden brown. Serve in soup plates. YUM!

Chicken Tangine—Morocco

Ingredients:

Rock salt
1 whole large chicken, cut into
8 pieces
1 tbsp. white vinegar
5 tbsp. olive oil
1 large bunch fresh cilantro,
chopped
1 tsp. cinnamon
½ tsp. real saffron
Pinch fine salt;
½ lb. onions, chopped
5 cloves garlic, chopped;
1 tsp. cumin
1 tsp. ground ginger;
1 tsp. paprika
1 tsp. turmeric;
¼ lb. gizzards, optional
¼ lb. chicken liver, optional;
¼ cup mixed olives, pitted
3 small preserved lemons

Method:

First rub the rock salt into the chicken pieces and then wash the chicken in the white vinegar and water.

Leave for 10 minutes. Rinse and dry and place onto a clean plate.

In a large bowl, mix the olive oil, coriander, cinnamon, saffron, fine salt, ½ the onions, garlic, cumin, ginger, paprika, turmeric.

Mix all these ingredients into the oil and crush the garlic and add a little water to make a paste.

Roll the chicken pieces into the marinade and leave for 10 to 15 minutes.

For cooking, use a tagine (traditional Moroccan dish) or a deep, heavy bottom casserole dish. Heat the dish up and add 2 tbsp. of olive oil to the hot dish.

Drop in the chicken and pour over the excess marinade juices.

Add the remaining onions, gizzards, chicken livers (if used), olives, and chopped preserved lemons (no pulp).

Cook in medium hot oven (350° F) for 45 minutes.

Serve with fresh bread.

Judy's Egyptian Chicken

Ingredients:

1 Whole Chicken
Vegetables
Rice
Spices to taste

Methods:

Dump a chicken into a big pot of boiling water with some salt and an onion. Boil for a couple hours. Fish out the chicken and set aside. Skim fat off the top of the soup. If you let this cool and skim it, you will have a fat free chicken stock. You now have the base for most of Egyptian cooking. Broth is used to flavor everything—especially vegetables, which are cooked in a mix of broth and tomato sauce. If you want to make a soup, there are 2 ways to do it, Egyptian style.

#1—Fry some orzo pasta (that little rice-shaped pasta you see in the grocery stores) in butter till browned, about 3-4 minutes. Add to soup and boil for another 5minutes. This is called sherba lisan asfour (swallows tongue soup) and is the most popular soup, at least with all the Egyptians I have met.

#2—If someone has been sick, a soup will be made by adding cut up zucchini, onion and other veggies, which is boiled till veggies are soft. This is called sherba hoodar (veggie soup). If you wanted to make a side dish of veggies, you would add the veggies to some broth, blend up tomatoes and strain the resulting liquid into the soup. You would use more tomato sauce than broth because you would want this to be a bit thick. I have seen peas and carrots and okra cooked this way a lot. Season to taste. The result is eaten spooned over rice. The chicken that was set aside would be browned in a frying pan and served with rice, soup and veggies. If you wanted to make a beef soup instead, just substitute meat for chicken but the meat broth is usually used as a base for mashi. Mashi is rice-stuffed veggies.

Garbanzo Stew

Ingredients:

1 tbsp. olive oil
1 cup finely chopped onion
4 cups chopped seeded
tomato (about 1½ lbs.)
1 tsp. sugar
1 tsp. curry powder
½ tsp. salt
¼ tsp. ground turmeric
1/8 tsp. ground red pepper
2 (15½-ounce) cans chickpeas
(garbanzo beans), drained
½ tsp. garam masala
¼ cup chopped fresh cilantro
Peanut Rice

Method:

Heat olive oil in a large saucepan over medium heat.

Add onion and sauté 5 minutes or until tender.

Stir in tomato and next 5 ingredients (tomato through pepper).

Cook 8 minutes or until thick, stirring occasionally.

Stir in chickpeas and garam masala; cook for 5 minutes or until thoroughly heated.

Sprinkle each serving with 1 tbsp. cilantro.

Serve over Peanut Rice.

Beef Stew with Vegetables—USA

Ingredients:

2 lbs. boneless beef stew meat
¼ cup all purpose flour
2 tbsp. canola or vegetable oil
1 cup mixture of chopped onions, green onions, green and red bell peppers
½ stalk of celery finely chopped
2 cloves minced garlic
1 cup green beans
Or 1 cup sweet corn

NOTE: for either vegetable you may substitute 1 can with juice or ½ package frozen.

Method:

1. First, in a large pot, combine the vegetables, broth, spice and sauces and heat over medium while browning the meat and making the roux.

2. In a skillet, brown the meat in 1 tbsp. of cooking oil and set aside.

3. Using the same skillet, add the remainder of oil and flour to make a bubbly paste. Over medium heat, let brown for 2 minutes and add chopped seasonings.

4. Continue cooking over medium heat until onions are opaque.

5. Add roux to pot with remainder of ingredients and bring to a boil. Stir well and lower heat to med-low setting. (You may have to add water to 1 inch above everything if too much liquid has been absorbed).

6.Continue cooking about 3½ hours or until meat is tender and gravy is thickened.

This great dish can be prepared with fresh, canned or frozen veggies or any combination of them! We love it served over white rice, but you could also serve it alone or over egg noodles. Enjoy!

Saira's Chilaquiles con Jocoqui
Mexican Lasagna with Sour Cream

Ingredients:

1 lb. homemade chorizo
18 corn tortillas, cut into
2-inch wide strips
2 cans red enchilada sauce
(Old El Paso or Ortega brand)
8 oz. Jack or Mild cheddar
cheese, grated
2 cups sour cream thinned
with ½ cup milk
1 cup extra sharp cheddar
1 sm. can sliced ripe black
olives, drained
2 green onions, thinly sliced

Method:

1. Cook the chorizo in a frying pan until the pink is gone. Set aside.

2. Spray a medium oblong baking dish with cooking spray. Pour in just enough enchilada sauce to thinly cover the bottom of the dish

3. Now start layering the ingredients: a layer of tortilla strips, some enchilada sauce, a sprinkling of chorizo, a sprinkling of Jack cheese. Then pour over a portion of the thinned sour cream. Repeat until the ingredients are used up.

4. Top with the 1 cup extra sharp cheddar, the sliced black olives, and the green onions.

5. Cover the baking dish tightly with foil and bake at 325° F for about 40 minutes. Let stand for 5-10 minutes to set before cutting into serving pieces.

NOTE: Chilaquiles is very much like a lasagna made with Mexican ingredients. Like lasagna, you can experiment with different styles of sauces, meats, vegetables, etc. This is my favorite version. It uses my Chorizo recipe (see page 118).

Umm Saddaqah Salmon Quiche

Ingredients:

1 pie crust (6 oz)
1 egg (optional)
1 packet of 2 salmon fillets
Dash of black pepper
1 packet of grated cheddar cheese or 2/3 of a bar of cheddar cheese grated
2/3 cup of milk or soy milk if preferred
2 tbsp. of flour
1 head of broccoli
almond essence (optional)
butter or margarine

Method:

In a skillet melt some butter or margarine. When it is all melted put in the salmon. Sauté the salmon until the color turns light pink. This should not take more than five minutes on a medium flame. Remove the salmon from the fire and place in a bowl large enough to hold the salmon and the chopped broccoli.

Cut up the broccoli using only the top two or three inches. In a skillet with a little butter sauté the broccoli with a few dashes of black pepper until the color of the broccoli changes to a bright green.

Remove the broccoli and put it in the bowl with the salmon.

Mix this up together but do it so that they are blended without the salmon being crushed.

Put in 2/3 of a cup of soy milk into a bowl. Add the egg and put some almond essence into this mixture.
Stir with a fork and put this into a skillet with a little butter over a low flame.
Fold 2 tbsp flour into this mixture. Remove from flame after the flour is folded into the mixture.

Cover the bottom of the pie crust with the grated cheese, not thick, but just to cover the bottom. Upon this place the salmon and the broccoli combination. Pour the milk, egg and flour mixture evenly over the mixed salmon and broccoli. Then cover this with some more grated cheese.

Preheat the oven to 350° F and bake for about 40 minutes, or until golden brown.

This serves 4, though you can add some vegetables to this as a side. It is not a lot of food but it is quite rich, so eat sparingly.

NOTE: The pie crust can be a graham type or a frozen crust. I prefer the graham crust. The salmon filet will come sometimes two to a packet, might be about 3 inches by 3 inches and about an inch thick. I use soy milk as opposed to regular milk. I don't always use an egg; sometimes I just use soy milk and whole wheat flour. If the salmon filet has skin on it just remove the skin and cut up the salmon into small squares. Season the salmon with black pepper and a pinch of salt if desired. You can also put in some almond essence, but this is optional.

Our Lord! Forgive us our sins as well as those of our brethren who proceeded us in faith and let not our hearts entertain any unworthy thoughts or feelings against [any of] those who have believed. Our Lord! You are indeed full of kindness and Most Merciful. (59:10)

Sleep-Cooking

—Corey Habbas—

I woke up unexpectedly at night
due to a craving with a bite
and in my hunger I did yearn
to sink my teeth into a loaf of sweet bread
spread with butter freshly churned.

Without even opening an eye
my hand clawed the refrigerator—none prepared
and half asleep I urged myself
to whip up a batch, as if by a dare.

I grabbed what felt like sugar and cream
but how could I have known?
It was like a dream!
Then I blended in the oil—I think,
or was it the soap on the side of the sink?
I added flour and cocoa powder
and a can of berries…or was it clam chowder?

As the concoction baked, it smelled so rank.
My dream into a nightmare sank
and my stomach growling ever stronger
meant that I couldn't wait much longer
to sink my teeth into that dish—
nor was it bread, nor so "delish".

Cajun Cassoulet

Ingredients:

¼ lb. halal meat, bacon style
1 medium onion, diced
1 green bell pepper, seeded
and diced
3 cloves garlic, minced
1 stalk celery, diced
2½ cups red beans (cooked
or canned)
1 tbsp tomato paste
2 cups chicken broth
½ lb. cooked chicken
(leftovers work well)
½ lb. Andouille (or smoked)
halal sausage, sliced
1 cup breadcrumbs (tossed
with 2 tbsp. melted butter)
1 tsp. Cajun seasoning blend

Method:

Render the meat in a heavy
skillet.

Remove the meat pieces.
Add the onion, bell pepper,
garlic, and celery.
Cook until just soft.

Add the beans, tomato paste,
meat pieces and broth.
Simmer for 15 minutes.

Pre-heat the oven to 350° F.

Lightly oil a medium
casserole dish. Place the meat
and sausage in the dish. Top
with the bean mixture. Cover
and bake for 30 minutes.

Toss the breadcrumbs,
butter, and Cajun seasonings
together. Top the casserole
with the mixture and bake
uncovered for 20 minutes or
until lightly browned.

The Holy Qur'an: 2:61 And remember ye said: "O
Moses! we cannot endure one kind of food (always); so
beseech thy Lord for us to produce for us of what the
earth growth, -its pot-herbs, and cucumbers, Its garlic,
lentils, and onions."

Curry Beef—India/Pakistan

Ingredients:

1 tbsp. curry powder
2 tbsp. low-sodium soy sauce
1 tbsp. rice vinegar
1 lb. beef eye-of-round roast, cut into thin strips
1 leek
1 tbsp. vegetable oil
1 tbsp. minced, peeled fresh ginger
4 garlic cloves, minced
1¼cups vertically sliced onion
½ tsp. white pepper
¼ tsp. salt
4 cups hot cooked rice

Method:

ESTIMATED TOTAL TIME: 45 minutes

Combine the first 4 ingredients in a medium bowl; cover and marinate in refrigerator 30 minutes.

Remove the roots, outer leaves, and tops from leek, leaving 1½ to 2 inches of dark leaves.

Rinse leeks with cold water, and cut into 2-inch julienne strips to yield 1¼ cups.

Heat oil in a large non-stick skillet over medium-high heat.

Add ginger and garlic; sauté 1½ minutes.

Add beef mixture; sauté 5 minutes.

Add leek, onion, pepper, and salt; sauté 3 minutes.

Serve over rice.

Saira's Machaca Burritos

Ingredients:

1½ to 2 lbs. boneless
chuck steak
2 tbsp. vegetable oil
2 tbsp. chili powder
6 cloves garlic, crushed
1 cup water
1 yellow onion,
coarsely chopped
1 bell pepper,
coarsely chopped
1 tbsp. vegetable oil
¼ cup pickled jalapenos,
chopped
6 eggs, beaten
black pepper, to taste
Habanero hot sauce or
Tabasco to taste
8 burrito size flour tortillas

Method:

1. Heat the vegetable oil in a skillet. (Make sure the skillet has a tight fitting lid to be used later in the recipe.) Sauté the crushed garlic (uncovered) for a few minutes, then add the chuck roast

2. Brown the roast well on both sides. Sprinkle with the chile powder, turn a couple of times to coat well, then add the water.

3. Lower the heat, cover, and braise the meat slowly for about 1 to 1½ hours, or until very tender. Check occasionally to make sure the water doesn't boil away. Add a little water, if necessary. (You can also do this part in a crock pot.)

4. With 2 forks, shred the beef and set aside.

5. In a clean skillet, heat the 1 Tbsp. vegetable oil, and sauté the onion and bell pepper. Add the chopped jalapenos.

6. Stir in the beaten eggs and scramble, then add the shredded beef. (If using a crock pot, add this to the meat rather than the other way around.)

7. Add black pepper and hot sauce to your taste.

8. Heat the tortillas briefly in the microwave. (About a minute for all 8.) Wrap a generous portion of the filling in each tortilla, and serve.

SERVINGS: Makes enough filling for 8 burritos

Saira's Pizza with Caramelized Onions and Portabello Mushrooms with Rosemary

Ingredients:

TOPPING:
2 tbsp. extra virgin olive oil
4-6 large cloves of garlic, thinly sliced
2 large onions, halved, then thinly sliced
3 large Portobello mushrooms, sliced into strips (or use a pound of sliced wild or crimini mushrooms—bland white mushrooms would be the last choice)
2 tsp. Balsamic vinegar
Hot red pepper flakes, to your taste
salt or seasoned salt to your taste
1 tbsp. fresh rosemary leaves (or 1 tsp. dried)
1 tbsp. tiny capers
2 cup shredded mozzarella or combination of your preferred cheeses

CRUST:
1 thick pizza crust (e.g. Boboli brand, original style. Thin style crusts will not be able to stand up to the heavy ingredients used in this pizza.)
1 tbsp. olive oil
2 cloves garlic, crushed
1 tsp. dried basil leaves

Method:

1. Heat about 2 tbsp. of the olive oil in a frying pan. When it becomes very fluid, add the onions and garlic to the pan. Stir-fry over a medium high heat until the onions begin to turn brown and get soft

2. Add the sliced mushrooms to the pan. Sprinkle with hot pepper flakes to your taste, salt or seasoned salt, and the rosemary. Lower the heat to medium and keep stirring gently, so as not to break up the mushrooms. They will want to stick a bit, but when they start releasing their water you will be able to stir up all the brown stuff from the bottom of the pan, and it will form a nice glaze over everything.

3. Sprinkle the Balsamic vinegar over the onions, garlic, and mushrooms and set aside, off the heat.

4. Spread the crust evenly with the remaining tablespoon of olive oil and the

crushed garlic. Then sprinkle the dried basil over it.

5. Spread the warm topping over the crust, and sprinkle with the capers and the cheese.

6. Bake in a preheated 450° F oven about 15 minutes, until the cheese is well melted and bubbly.

From "101 Tales My Grandmother Used To Tell"

—Nancy E. Biddle—

My grandmother married an adventurous young Englishman who had a store in Leon, Nicaragua. She went off to Nicaragua with him and though life was difficult and lonely for her, there were high moments where she had the chance to hob-nob with British upper class stationed in Managua, the capital city. At one such event the hostess had imported a plump duck from the USA and had it roasted to a golden turn. The presentation was superb and the cooks brought it into the dining room with a bit too much gusto. The serving girl slipped. The duck and all the fixings flew onto the floor. She stood up in absolute horror, but the hostess was full of poise.

"Maria," she called out raising her hand in a forgiving gesture, "Just bring in the other duck!"

"Of course! I will!" Maria said, instantly rescued, and she and her entourage scooped up the duck and disappeared into the kitchen.

She came out a few minutes later with the other duck even more beautiful than the first, and all the guests hungrily devoured it. It was only later that the truth came out about the other duck. In fact, there had only been one. Maria simply redressed it.

From then on, of course, when any meal time upset happened, somebody would always chime in, "Just bring in the other duck!" My grandmother was full of stories; this was one of my favourites.

Karen's Chicken Parmesan—Italy

Ingredients:

4 - 6 chicken breasts
some grated Parmesan or
Romano cheese (I guess you
could substitute whatever
kind of cheese you want—
and I forgot to write down
how much, but I guess...
enough to sprinkle heavily
over the dish after it's prepared)
1 bag of field peas with snaps
(frozen food section kind)
2 cans of chopped tomatoes
with jalapenos
2 tbsp of olive oil (oh darn! I
should have put this one in
the Olive Oil book too—oh
well!)
5 cloves of fresh garlic,
smashed and then chopped
½ tsp. of sea salt
1 tsp. fresh ground black
pepper (or to taste)
½ tsp. cumin

Method:

Cover the bottom of a
casserole dish with the
olive oil and garlic

Lay the chicken pieces on top
of the oil/garlic and sprinkle
with salt and pepper

Spread peas/beans (snaps)
and tomatoes over the top of
the chicken

Bake covered at 375° for 45
minutes

Uncover, sprinkle with
Parmesan cheese and cumin

Bake for an additional 20
minutes uncovered.

SERVINGS: Four to six.

The Holy Qur'an: 2:25 But give glad tidings to those
who believe and work righteousness, that their portion
is Gardens, beneath which rivers flow. Every time they
are fed with fruits therefrom, they say: "Why, this is
what we were fed with before," for they are given
things in similitude; and they have therein Companions
pure and holy; and they abide therein forever.

Asian Stuffed Peppers

Ingredients:

2½ ounces uncooked curly
Chinese-style noodles or
angel hair pasta, broken
into thirds
2 large red bell peppers
1 cup cubed firm tofu (about
6 ounces)
2 tbsp. hoisin sauce
1 tbsp. low-sodium soy sauce
2 tsps. dark sesame oil
2 garlic cloves, minced
½ cup diagonally sliced
snow peas
½ cup (1½-inch) julienne-cut
carrot
2 tbsp. chopped fresh cilantro

Method:

1. Cook noodles according to package directions, omitting salt and fat; drain.

2. Cut each bell pepper in half lengthwise, and discard seeds and membranes. Arrange pepper halves in a 9-inch pie plate. Cover with heavy-duty plastic wrap. Microwave at high 5 minutes or until crisp-tender; drain. Return peppers to pie plate.

3. Combine tofu, hoisin sauce, and soy sauce in a small bowl; set aside. Heat oil in a non-stick skillet over medium-high heat. Add garlic; sauté 15 seconds. Add peas and carrot; sauté 3 minutes or until vege-tables are tender. Add tofu mixture; sauté for 1 minute or until thoroughly heated. Stir in noodles. Divide noodle mixture evenly among pepper halves; sprinkle each pepper half with 1½ tsps. cilantro.

SERVINGS: Four

Chicken and Broccoli
Bowtie Pasta With An Asian Flair

This is a great "quick and easy" meal that can be prepared in a flash!

Ingredients:

1 package bowtie noodles
½ cup low sodium soy sauce
2 tbsp. Teriyaki sauce
1 can chicken broth
4 boneless, skinless chicken breasts cut into large squares
1½ tbsp. cornstarch
1 package frozen broccoli florets
1 tbsp. toasted sesame seeds
1 tbsp. canola cooking oil

Method:

1. First, boil the noodles as per package directions and set aside.

2. Mix the soy sauce, chicken broth, teriyaki and cornstarch in a separate bowl and set aside.

3. In a large wok or deep skillet, cook the chicken in the cooking oil until no longer pink.

4. Add the frozen broccoli and liquid mixture and continue cooking on med/high heat for about 6 - 8 more minutes or until broccoli and sauce are heated through.

5. Finally, add the cooked noodles and sesame seeds and mix well.

6. Remove from heat and enjoy a great easy meal!

Green Chile and Chicken Enchiladas

Ingredients:

1 whole chicken and stock
24 corn tortillas
1 can cream of chicken soup
1 can cream of mushroom soup
1 medium onion, finely chopped
1 lb. of longhorn natural cheese, grated
Olive Oil for coating corn tortillas (approximately 1 cup needed)
2 cans of chopped green chile or 12 fresh green chile finely chopped

Method:

Boil the chicken until tender, remove from pot and cool, remove skin, debone and separate into bite size pieces.

Place chicken soup and mushroom soup in a large cooking pot.

Add the chopped onion and chile. Add chicken pieces. Add chicken stock: 1 to 2 cups.

Heat until this mixture is warm. Pour olive oil in a skillet and heat it to warm temperature

In a deep baking dish cover the bottom of the dish with the chicken mixture.

Then using tongs dip a corn tortilla in the warm olive oil and then place it on the chicken mixture.

Continue this procedure until the first layer covers the mixture. Sprinkle grated cheese over the first layer of chicken mixture and corn tortillas.

Spoon the chicken mixture over the layer of corn tortillas.

Continue layering chicken mixture, tortillas and cheese until all corn tortillas are used.

Cover baking dish with aluminum foil and bake at 325° F for 30-45 minutes or until corn tortillas are soft and moist.

Cinnamon Lamb Chops—Middle East

Ingredients:

4 to 6 medium lamb chops
2 medium tomatoes
1 onion
2 tbsp Cumin (black seeds if you have them)
Pinch of salt
black pepper (as desired)
2 tbsp cinnamon (more or less as desired)
¼ to ½ cup of water

Method:

Place lamb chops in a deep-dish baking pan.

Cut tomatoes in small wedges. Slice onion.

Sprinkle salt, black pepper, cumin and cinnamon evenly on top of the lamb chops.

Add cut tomatoes and onion slices.

Add ¼ to ½ cup of water. Cover the dish in aluminum foil.

Bake at 325° F (depending on your oven) until lamb chops are tender.

Chicken legs can be substituted for the lamb chops. Boil them in water first and remove the skin when they are about ½ cooked. Substitute the chicken stock for the water.

Serve with brown rice and a green salad.

SERVINGS: Four to six.

Grilled Salmon

Ingredients:

12 ounces salmon filets
3 tbsps butter, softened
1 tsp. lemon juice
½ tsp. lemon zest
(grated peel)
1 tsp. chives, fresh, chopped
1 tsp. parsley, fresh, chopped

Method:

Place the butter, lemon juice, zest, and herbs in a food processor. Pulse until just blended.

Place in parchment paper or plastic wrap. Roll into a cylinder.

Refrigerate for at least 30 minutes.

Cut the salmon into two portions and grill.

Cut the butter into ¼-inch circles.

Place the salmon on plates and immediately top with the butter circles.

Serve immediately.

Our Lord! In You we have placed our trust, and to You do we turn in repentance, for unto You is the end of all journeys. (60:4)

Cooking With Kids

—Pamela K. Taylor—

Cooking—stirring, baking, folding, braising, boiling,
whipping, mashing, kneading, blending, broiling,
frying, roasting, mixing, grilling, beating
whisking, steaming, tossing, rolling, heating

With—joint, together, side by side
associate, cooperate, unified

Kids—daughter, son, child, offspring, progeny,
teenager, toddler, youth, descendant, family

Cooking with Kids?
fun, friendly, messy, silly, thrilling
joyful, jumbled, sloppy, slurpy, spilling,
tasting, testing, poking, prodding, sharing
laughing, smiling, singing, hugging, caring

Judy's Egyptian Beef-Potatoes

Ingredients:

4-5 large potatoes
2-3 onions
2-3 green peppers
Several ripe tomatoes
or you can cheat and use the
canned stuff
beef—as much or little as you
like, sliced into smallish pieces
seasonings: salt, pepper, garlic
powder, cumin, fresh dill and
cilantro

Method:

Into a baking dish place slices
of potato, slices of onion,
peppers and beef.

Sprinkle with salt, pepper,
cumin, if desired and garlic
powder.

In a blender, add washed and
chopped tomatoes with the
rest of the onion, and fresh
herbs, like dill and cilantro.

Whirl into a sauce and strain
into the baking dish of beef
and vegetables.

If you like the seeds and stuff
and your kids will eat them,
just dump the whole thing
into the dish.

Toss veggies and beef to coat,
cover and put into the oven at
350° for about an hour and a
half.

If you do not cover, you will
have to add some water to the
dish to prevent it from drying
out.

Serve with rice and a salad.

This is a versatile dish. I use
whatever veggies I happen to
have on hand. Carrots would
go nicely and peas. I have
used squash and zucchini as
well.

SERVINGS: Varies

Shrimp and Fennel Sauce for Pasta

Ingredients:

Big pinch of red pepper flakes
2 tsp. olive oil
1 fennel bulb, trimmed, cored
and thinly sliced
¼ tsp. fennel seed, optional
2 cups your favorite jarred
tomato sauce
8 oz. peeled medium shrimp

Method:

Heat oil in a saucepan over
medium heat

Add sliced fennel and cook
until soft, about 7 minutes.

Stir in fennel seed, if using,
and red pepper flakes.

Cook for 1 minute.

Add tomato sauce and sim-
mer for 5 minutes to blend
flavors.

Add shrimp; simmer until
pink and warmed through.

Serve over your favorite pasta.

ESTIMATED COOKING TIME:
under 30 minutes

The Holy Qur'an 16:14 It is He Who has made the sea
subject, that ye may eat thereof flesh that is fresh and
tender, and that ye may extract therefrom ornaments
to wear; and thou seest the ships therein that plough
the waves, that ye may seek (thus) of the bounty of
Allah and that ye may be grateful.

Side Dishes

Judy's Baba Ghanoush—Egypt

Ingredients:

2 large purple eggplants
salt to taste
cumin to taste
2 tsp. tahini
olive oil

Method:

Place the eggplants on a cookie sheet in the oven at 350° for about an hour. They will get soft and the skins will split.

Scoop out the pulp into a bowl and mash it up. A food processor would do it quicker if you have one.

Sprinkle a bit of salt and cumin on the eggplant and add a couple teaspoons of tahini (sesame paste-which can be bought in any Middle Eastern grocery store) and drizzle some olive oil over it.

Mix well.

Can be eaten either hot or cold and goes well with warm pita bread. I have substituted a low-fat Italian dressing for the olive oil and I prefer this.

Couscous and Feta Cakes—Morocco

Couscous, tiny pasta usually found with the rice and grains, makes a wonderful foundation to go with tangy cheese and sweet bell peppers. Serve with a romaine salad tossed with cucumbers, tomatoes, kalamata olives, and lemon.

Ingredients:

2½ cups water
1 cup uncooked couscous
4 tsps. olive oil, divided
1 cup minced red onion
1 cup minced red bell pepper
½ cup minced green bell pepper
2 garlic cloves, minced
1 (4-ounce) package crumbled Feta cheese
1/2 cup all-purpose flour
1/2 cup egg substitute
2 tbsp. minced fresh parsley
1/4 tsp. salt
1/4 tsp. white pepper

Method:

PREP TIME: 10 minutes
COOKING TIME: 15 minutes

Bring water to a boil in a small saucepan; stir in couscous.

Remove from heat; cover and let stand 10 minutes. Fluff with a fork.

Place 1 tsp. oil in an electric skillet; heat to 375° F.

Add onion, bell peppers, and garlic; sauté 5 minutes.

Combine couscous, onion mixture, cheese, and remaining ingredients in a large bowl; stir well.

Place ½ tsp. oil in skillet; heat to 375° F.

Place 1/3 cup couscous mixture for each of 4 portions into skillet, shaping each portion into a 3-inch cake in the skillet.

Cook 6 minutes or until golden brown, turning cakes carefully after 3 minutes.

Remove cakes and keep warm.

Repeat procedure with remaining oil and couscous mixture.

Chinese Fried Rice

This is a very simple Asian dish. Just like making sandwiches, so many combinations to choose from. Just be creative!

1. Use leftover cooked rice, or cook rice then store in the fridge for 3-4 hrs or preferably overnight. Doing this separates the grains of the cooked rice.

2. Prepare an omelet, and chop it into pieces.

3. Chop some garlic. Use as much as you like, the more the better!

4. ½ inch stem ginger—peeled and chopped (optional)

5. Cooking oil—2 tbsp. or more according to taste.

6. Carrots OR cabbage OR green/red pepper bells OR any vegetables that you fancy! 'Crunchy veggies' are preferred. Chop them all up! (Four carrots, chopped real small, otherwise boil them half cooked if you don't like that raw carrot taste in your fried rice.)

7. Chop some halal sausage or any leftover meat/chicken as long as they are cooked!

8. Soy Sauce—about 2 to5 tsp. (optional)

9. Sesame oil—to taste (optional)

10. A wok is preferable, otherwise just use a frying pan. Heat about 2 tbsp. of oil (any oil). Sauté the garlic and ginger. Add in rice, veggies and meat and keep 'tossing' them together. Add in chopped omelet and Soy sauce. Salt to taste.

For myself, I like to add in chopped spring onions at the last moment. For the health conscious, olive oil is also suitable—the more the better.

Smoked Gouda and Onion Quiche

Ingredients:

1 tbsp. butter
½ medium onion, diced
1 deep-dish pie shell (frozen)
¾ cup smoked gouda cheese, grated
4 eggs
1½ cups half and half (light cream)
1½ tsp. parsley, chopped
dash white pepper
1/8 tsp. salt

Method:

Pre-heat the oven to 375° F.

Melt the butter in a small skillet.

Add the onions and cook until just soft. Set aside.

Bake the empty pie shell for 5 minutes.

Remove from the oven and place it on a cookie sheet.

Place the cheese in the bottom of the warm shell.

In a mixing bowl, lightly beat the eggs.

Whisk in the half and half, parsley, onions, and seasonings.

Pour into the shell.

Bake for 25-35 minutes, or until the pie is firm.

Serve this delicious savory pie, warm or chilled, at your next brunch.

SERVINGS: 6

The Prophet said, "Nobody has ever eaten a better meal than that which one has earned by working with one's own hands. The Prophet of Allah, David used to eat from the earnings of his manual labor." (Hadith by Bukhari, Volume 3, Book 34, Number 286)

Baked Rice

Ingredients:

2 cups of rice
2 cups of milk-skim to heavy
cream—it does not matter
about 3-4 tbsp. of butter

Method:

Put rice into a casserole dish.
Add the milk and butter.
Place into a 350° F. oven until
the top is golden brown or
about 45 minutes to an hour.

SERVINGS: Varies.

NOTE: You can make this recipe bigger; just add 1 cup of milk for every cup of rice and a little more butter. Be sure to put the dish on a cookie sheet or you will have to clean your oven.

I have substituted broth for the milk and added onions and peas and carrots and it came out really well also. I used half a bag of frozen peas and carrots and added a half a cup more broth. If the broth is seasoned, no need to add more but if not, then season to taste.

Our Lord! You embrace all things within Your
Grace and Knowledge, forgive those who repent
and follow Your path, and ward off from them
the punishment of Hell. (40:7)

Tortilla Espanola (Spanish Potato Omelet)

Tortilla Espanola (its relation to Mexican tortillas comes solely from its round shape) is among the most popular dishes in Spain. Although its ingredients couldn't be more basic—potatoes, eggs, onions, and oil—they're combined and cooked in a way that makes this dish irresistible and versatile. The potatoes are normally fried, but we've roasted them with excellent results. Unlike American omelets, this one's best made several hours ahead then served at room temperature.

Ingredients:

6 cups thinly sliced peeled baking potato (about 3 lbs.)
2 cups thinly sliced sweet onion
cooking spray
2 tbsp. olive oil, divided
¾ tsp. kosher salt, divided
4 large eggs
oregano sprigs (optional)

Method:

Preheat oven—350° F.

Place the potato and onion in a roasting pan coated with cooking spray. Drizzle with 1 tbsp. plus 2 tsps. oil, and sprinkle with 1/2 tsp. salt. Toss well.

Bake at 350° F. for 1 hour or until potatoes are tender, stirring occasionally with a metal spatula to prevent sticking.

Combine eggs and ¼ tsp. salt in a large bowl. Stir in potato mixture; let stand 10 minutes.

Heat 1 tsp. oil in an 8-inch nonstick skillet over medium heat.

Pour potato mixture into pan (pan will be very full). Cook 7 minutes or until almost set, gently shaking pan frequently.

Place a plate upside down on top of omelet; invert onto plate. Carefully slide omelet cooked side up into pan; cook 3 minutes or until set, gently shaking pan occasionally.

Carefully loosen omelet with a spatula; gently slide omelet onto a plate. Cool. Cut into wedges.

Stewed Red Cabbage With a German Flavor

This recipe was passed down from a friend who spent some time in Germany on an Army base and brought this wonderfully easy and delicious dish home! Even for non-cabbage lovers (like myself), this dish is great!

Ingredients:

1 head purple/red cabbage, chopped
1 8-10 oz. bottle "Catalina" French salad dressing
3 strips uncooked turkey bacon
1/3 tsp. ground ginger
1/3 tsp. black pepper
½ tsp. onion or garlic powder
2 tbsp. cooking oil

Method:

First, heat the oil in a large covered saucepan or pot.

Fry the turkey bacon until done (not crispy)

Add the cabbage, cover and cook on medium heat for about 5 minutes.

Add the dressing and other spices, cover and continue cooking until cabbage is "cooked down" (about 10 minutes)

Serve as a side dish or add halal sausage and enjoy as your main course!

The Holy Qur'an 6:14—It is He Who produceth gardens, with trellises and without, and dates, and tilth with produce of all kinds, and olives and pomegranates, similar (in kind) and different (in variety): eat of their fruit in their season.

Egyptian Fool

This is a fava bean dish ubiquitous to the Middle East. It's eaten for breakfast, late dinners and snacks. Here in Egypt vendors go around with a big cauldron of the beans and sell them. You add spices when you get it home. In the US, you can buy cans of fava beans in any Middle Eastern grocery store.

Methods:

1) Dump the beans (and their liquid) in a small pan and heat over a medium low flame as the beans are already cooked. What you want to do is reduce them to a refried bean consistency.

After about 7 minutes or so, mash with a fork; the liquid should start to thicken.

Add a couple tsps. of tahini, some garlic powder and some salt to taste and mix well.

When it looks like refried beans, spoon it into a plate.

Drizzle olive oil on top of this—not too much, maybe a tablespoon's worth.

2) For breakfast, this would be eaten with bread, accompanied by sliced cucumber, tomatoes, pickled veggies called turshi (usually turnips, carrots, onion, cucumber and lemon) and eggs—hardboiled or scrambled, and halawa (a sweet made of sugar and ground sesame seeds—either with pistachio nuts or without).

3)Spoon this into a pita and you have a favorite sandwich. This would be equivalent to a McDonalds' hamburger in the USA. You could also use this as a bean dip for chips.

NOTE: During Ramadan here in Egypt, the Egyptian Fool is eaten every night with Iftar (the meal which breaks the fast). It is very nutritious and filling. If you made Baba Ghanoush, eat this with it as well.

The Five Pillars of Islam

The Declaration of Faith.

"I bear witness that there is no one worthy of worship except God (Allah), and that Muhammad is His servant and messenger."

Prayers

Prayers are prescribed five times a day as a duty toward God. Prayer strengthens and enlivens belief in God and inspires man to higher morality. It purifies the heart and controls temptation, wrong-doing, and evil.

Fasting

Fasting during the month of Ramadan means abstention from food, beverages, and sex from dawn to sunset, and curbing evil intentions and desires. It teaches love, sincerity, and devotion. It develops patience, unselfishness, social conscience, and willpower to bear hardship.

Zakah

Zakah is a proportionately fixed contribution collected from the wealth and earnings of the well to do and rich. It is spent on the poor and needy in particular, and the welfare of the society in general. The payment of Zakah purifies ones income and wealth and helps to establish economic balance and social justice in the society.

Hajj

Hajj, or pilgrimage to the Ka'bah in Makkah, once in a lifetime, is required, provided one has the means to undertake the journey.

Desserts and Baking

Saira's—Karla's Mom's
German Chocolate Candy Balls

Ingredients:

4½ cups crushed graham crackers
Rind of 1 lemon, grated
2 whole eggs
2 egg yolks
1 lb. butter
2 lbs. powdered sugar
1¼ cup unsweetened cocoa powder
1 or 1½ cups finely chopped walnuts, pecans, or toasted hazelnuts
Colored sugar crystals
(Get the large size in the little plastic bowls. Makes for convenient rolling later.)

Method:

Combine all the ingredients, except sugar crystals, in a bowl. Mix and knead thoroughly. Be brave. It will take a long time and you will get tired. Rest occasionally.

NOTE: You will need an enormous bowl to mix this in. A dough bowl is a good choice. Get in there with your hand to mix because the dough is very stiff. Use only ONE hand, though, otherwise you'll never get loose!

When you have a homogenous mixture, form into balls the size of walnuts and roll in the sugar sprinkles (kids love to do this part—get yours to help you!). Or form into 4 logs and roll in the sprinkles, then slice ¼ inch thick to serve.

Store in an air-tight tin or Tupperware. These might keep a long time if everyone didn't eat them up so fast! These need no refrigeration.

Chocolate Carrot Slice

Ingredients:

1 cup self-raising flour
1 tsp. ground cinnamon
¾ cup caster sugar
½ cup finely grated carrot
1 cup mixed dried fruit
½ cup chocolate bits or chocolate chips
1/3 cup desiccated (dried) coconut;
2 eggs, lightly beaten
90g unsalted butter, melted;
1/3 cup chopped walnuts

CREAM CHEESE FROSTING:
125 g cream cheese
30 g unsalted butter
1½ cups icing sugar, sifted;
1 tsp. hot water

Method:

Preheat oven to moderate 180° C. Brush a shallow 23 cm square cake tin with melted butter or oil and line the base and sides with baking paper.

1. Sift flour and cinnamon into a large mixing bowl. Add caster sugar, grated carrot, mixed dried fruit, chocolate bits and desiccated coconut and stir until just combined.

Add beaten eggs and melted butter. Stir until the mixture is just combined.

2. Spread mixture evenly into prepared tin and smooth surface. Bake for 30 minutes or until golden. Cool in tin; turn out.

CREAM CHEESE FROSTING: Using electric beaters, beat cream cheese and butter in small mixing bowl until smooth.

Add icing sugar and beat for 2 minutes or until mixture is light and fluffy. Add water; beat until combined.

Spread slice with frosting using a flat-bladed knife and sprinkle with walnuts. Cut accordingly.

STORAGE: Keep in an airtight container and store, preferably in the fridge. It can be stored for 2 months in the freezer (without icing).

HINT: Sprinkle the cream cheese frosting with grated chocolate if desired. This slice is also delicious without icing.

Maple Pumpkin Pie—USA

Ingredients:

1¼ c maple syrup
1 tsp. salt
4 large eggs
1 29-oz. can of unseasoned
pumpkin
20 oz. evaporated milk
(1 12-oz. can and 1 8-oz. can.)
2 9-inch deep dish unbaked
pie shells (4 cup volume) OR
4 9-inch shallow unbaked pie
shells (2 cup volume)
You can also use a graham
cracker crust.

Spice Mix:

OPTION A:
1 tbsp. to 2 tbsp. store bought
pumpkin pie spice

OPTION B:
2 tsp. to 1 tbsp. ground
cinnamon
1 tsp. to 1½ tsp. ground
ginger
½ tsp. to ¾ tsp. ground cloves
1/8 to ¼ tsp. allspice

Method:

Mix: maple syrup, salt, spice
mix, in small bowl. Set aside.

Beat: 4 eggs in large bowl

Stir in: syrup and spice mix
into eggs.

Stir in: pumpkin into egg mix.

Gradually stir in: evaporated
milk.

Pour: into pie shells.

Bake: 425° F for 15 minutes.
Reduce temperature to 350° F.

Continue Baking: 4 cup
volume pie shells for 40-50
minutes, until knife inserted
near center comes out clean.
2 cup volume pie shells for
20-30 minutes, until knife
inserted near center comes
out clean.

Cool: on wire rack, 90 minutes to 2 hours.

Serve immediately after cool-
ing OR refrigerate.

Pound Cake—USA

Sour cream adds a nice kick to this old favorite.

Ingredients:

4 ounces butter, softened
3 cups sugar
4 eggs
2 cups flour
½ tsp. baking powder
½ cup sour cream
1 tsp. vanilla extract

Method:

Place the butter and sugar in a mixer. Cream until smooth.

Add the eggs—one at a time with the mixer running.

In a separate bowl, sift together the flour and baking powder.

Blend well into the egg mixture.

Add the sour cream and vanilla and mix until blended.

Pre-heat the oven to 325° F.

Grease and flour a bread pan.
Pour in the batter.
Bake for 55-60 minutes.

Allow the cake to cool before serving.

Mandarin Cream Delight—USA

Ingredients:

CRUST:
9 tbsp. butter or stick
margarine, softened
½ cup sugar
1 tsp. vanilla extract
1½ cups all-purpose flour
1/8 tsp. salt
cooking spray

FILLING:
2 (11-ounce) cans mandarin
oranges in light syrup,
undrained
¼ cup sugar
1 (16-ounce) carton fat-free
sour cream
1 (8-ounce) carton low-fat
sour cream
2 (3.4-ounce) packages
vanilla instant pudding mix
or 2 (1.4-ounce) packages
sugar-free vanilla instant
pudding mix
1 (8-ounce) container frozen
reduced-calorie whipped
topping, thawed
Mint sprigs (optional)

Method:

CRUST:
To prepare crust, combine
the butter, ½ cup sugar, and
vanilla in a large bowl.

Beat at medium speed of a
mixer until light and fluffy
(about 2 minutes).

Lightly spoon flour into dry
measuring cups; level with a
knife.

Add flour and salt to butter
mixture, beating at low speed
until well-blended.

Preheat oven to 400° F.

Pat dough into a 13 x 9-inch
baking dish coated with cooking spray, and pierce through
to the bottom of dough with a
fork.

Bake at 400° F for 12 minutes
or until lightly browned.

Cool crust on a wire rack.

FILLING:
To prepare filling, drain mandarin oranges over a large bowl, reserving ½ cup juice.

Combine juice, ¼ cup sugar, sour cream, and pudding mix in a large bowl.

Stir in the orange segments. Spoon orange mixture over crust, spreading evenly.

Top with whipped topping. Chill 1 hour.

"If Allah brings you to it,
He will bring you through it.
Happy moments, praise Allah.
Difficult moments, seek Allah.
Quiet moments, worship Allah.
Painful moments, trust Allah.
Every moment, thank Allah."
—Author Unknown—

Salaam Suhoor Saffron Bread

This versatile sweet bread recipe comes out of the oven soft and aromatic and can be eaten with fruit, cheese or a side of whipped honey butter.

Ingredients:

4 tsps. dry yeast
1 cup granulated sugar
10 strands of saffron
1 cup milk
3 eggs
6 cups flour (approximate)
1 tsp. salt
½ cup butter
¼ cup cream cheese
1 tbsp of olive oil
more water (as needed)
zest of one large orange
2 tbsp. granulated sugar
powdered sugar (to taste)
1 egg yolk
2 tbsp. milk

Method:

Place sugar and milk in a bowl and microwave on medium heat for one minute or until warm enough to activate the yeast but not hot enough to destroy it. Stir and set aside for 5 minutes.

In a large mixing bowl, beat the cream cheese, butter, oil, eggs and salt until smooth. Pour in the yeast mixture. Using a wooden spoon stir in 2½ cups of flour. Dough should be like a batter, very loose and sticky. Cover with plastic wrap and a light towel and let rise for 2 hours.

Place orange zest in a food processor and mince as small as possible, gradually adding 2 tbsp. of sugar.

Uncover the dough and add the zest mixture, stirring until well blended. Next, using a wooden spoon, stir the rest of the flour in, ½ cups at a time until all of it has incorporated into the dough. If too dry, then add water, 1 tbsp. at a time until it is a good consistency. It will still be too sticky to squeeze at this point. Cover and let rise another 2 hours.

Preheat oven to 325° F Using a rubber spatula, scrape the dough onto a four dusted bread board and knead briefly. Cut dough and shape it into 5 inch round buns. You may also cut 2-inch by 5-inch strips and braid the dough. Set them on lightly greased cookie sheets.

In a small bowl, whisk the egg yolk and 2 tbsp. of milk. Using a small kitchen brush, paint the top of each dough loaf with the yolk glaze. Bake for 25-30 minutes or until done.

Best when eaten warm.

SERVINGS: 8

A Cake for Mama

—Nicole Bovey Alhakawati—

"Look, Mama! I made you a cake!" The baking pan held something dark and uneven, burnt on one side and thick on the other.

"What do you think, Mama?"

"Well," I began. Then I noticed the cake mix box perched on top of a moving box. The mix was more than half full.

"Is this the cake mix you used, Honey?"

"Yeah, Yayah helped me read the directions! And we even cleaned up!"

I tried not to laugh, but I couldn't help it. I grabbed my daughter in a bear hug and laughed till I cried. I had been unavailable to her the past few weeks with our Hijra to a new country. My lovely six-year-old had enlisted the help of our brand-new maid, who knew little to no English, to help her do what I couldn't. SubhanAllah.

"Who wants some cake?" I called. "Now we just have to find some plates!"

Banana-Date Flaxseed Bread

Ingredients:

½ cup flaxseeds
2/3 cup mashed ripe banana
½ cup sugar
¼ cup vegetable oil
2 large eggs
1½ cups all-purpose flour
¼ cup flaxseeds
½ tsp. baking powder
½ tsp. baking soda
½ tsp. salt
½ cup whole pitted dates, chopped
cooking spray

Method:

Place ½ cup flaxseeds in a blender, and process until ground to measure ¾ cup flaxseed meal. Set flaxseed meal aside.

Preheat oven to 350° F.

Beat the banana, sugar, oil, and eggs at medium speed of a mixer until well-blended.

Lightly spoon flour into dry measuring cups, and level with a knife.

Combine flour, flaxseed meal, ¼ cup flaxseeds, baking powder, baking soda, and salt, and gradually add to sugar mixture, beating until well-blended.

Stir in chopped dates.

Spoon the batter into an 8 x 4-inch loaf pan coated with cooking spray.

Bake bread at 350° F for 55 minutes or until a wooden pick inserted in center comes out clean.

Cool 10 minutes in pan on a wire rack, and remove from pan. Cool completely on wire rack.

Healthy Bran Rusks

Ingredients:

6 cups flour
10 tsp. baking powder
2 cups brown sugar
4 cups All Bran flakes
1 cup sunflower seeds or ½ sunflower and ½ oats
1 cup muesli (flavor of your choice)
1 cup pecan nuts/walnuts, cut up
¼ cup fennel seeds
¼ cup sesame seeds
½ cup dates cut up
500g margarine/butter melted
3 eggs beaten
500 ml sour milk

Method:

Combine all dry ingredients in a bowl.

Mix the sour milk and beaten eggs. Add all at once with the melted butter to the dry ingredients.

Mix lightly until combined. Do not over handle dough.

Pat into two greased oven roasters (28cm x 35cm).

Bake at 180° C until done.

Remove from oven and allow to cool in the pan.

Cut into 2cm wide fingers.

Turn out onto trays and return to 100° C oven to dry or leave in warming drawer overnight. When cool, pack into airtight tins.

Koeksusters—South Africa

Koeksusters are a South African favorite. Thought to be a Cape Malay invention, they are enjoyed by all. The closest equivalent in American terms would be a doughnut, except that these are spiced and dipped in syrup once fried and covered in a generous sprinkling of desiccated coconut.

Ingredients:

4 cups flour
2 tsp. powdered cinnamon
1 tsp. powdered ginger
½ tsp. nutmeg
¼ tsp. cloves
¼ tsp. ground cardamom
(optional)
¼ sup sugar
1 sachet instant dried yeast
(10g)
2 eggs
1 cup milk warmed
2 tbsp. condensed milk
1 large or two small potatoes
boiled and mashed
2 tbsp. butter

SYRUP:
Combine 2 cups sugar and 2 cups water in a saucepan.

Stir over low heat to dissolve the sugar.

Boil until a slightly sticky syrup is formed.

Method:

Combine dry ingredients in a bowl.

Mix the mashed potato (no lumps must remain in the potato), butter, condensed milk, eggs and warm milk.

Add this to the dry ingredients.

Mix to combine, adding extra warm water if necessary.

Form into a soft dough and knead thoroughly.

Transfer into an oiled plastic container with a tight fitting lid.

Place in a warm place until doubled in bulk.

Divide dough into 36 balls. Shape into ovals and flatten between your hands.

Place on oiled or floured trays.

Leave to rise once more, covered under a sheet of plastic.

Heat oil and fry each to a dark brown.

Drain on kitchen towels. Dip in the warm syrup and sprinkle generously with desiccated coconut.

Serve warm.

NOTE: Leftover koeksusters can be frozen or kept for later. To serve, sprinkle with a bit of water, wrap in foil and heat in the oven. Syrup them as explained, and enjoy.

Saira's Aunt Esther's Apple Cake—USA

This recipe was given to me by my Aunt Esther, who missed her calling when she never opened a bakery! She is justly famous in our family for her amazing baked treats.

Ingredients:

4 cup peeled, cored, diced apples (Golden Delicious or Galas)
2 cup sugar

In a medium bowl, pour the sugar over the diced apples and stir. Let the apples stand for about an hour before you proceed with the rest of the recipe.

2 eggs
½ cup vegetable oil
2 tsp. vanilla extract
2 tsp. baking soda
2 tsp. cinnamon
1 tsp. salt
2 cup flour
½ cup cocoa powder, sifted
1 cup chopped walnuts
powdered sugar to sift over cake.

Method:

In a large bowl, beat the eggs slightly, then beat in the oil and vanilla.

Mix and sift the dry ingredients. Stir in all together with the egg-oil mixture and the apple-sugar mixture. Stir by hand, don't use a mixer.

Stir in the nuts

Pour into a prepared bundt cake pan. Bake at 350° F for about 1 hour.

Cool 10 minutes, then remove from pan.

When completely cool, sift powdered sugar over the cake.

NOTE: This cake keeps well. It mellows nicely after the first day. It also freezes well.

Charlotte Russe

It's time to rediscover this classic dessert.

Ingredients:

¼ cup water
1 envelope unflavored halal gelatin
½ cup milk
½ cup sugar
1½ tsp. vanilla
1 cup cream
Ladyfingers or sliced sponge cake

Method:

Add the water to a saucepan.

Sprinkle on the gelatin. Allow to rest for 5 minutes.

Whisk in the milk and sugar. Over low heat, heat the mixture, stirring constantly, until it begins to thicken.

Remove from the heat and add the vanilla. Chill.

Whip until firm peaks form.

In a separate bowl, whip the cream until firm peaks form.

Fold the two mixtures until blended.

Line a 1½ quart dish with the ladyfingers (bottom and sides).

Pour in the mixture. Chill well.

Un-mold or serve with a spoon.

Buttermilk Pudding

This is a wonderful, light pudding, perfect for chilly winter days. Serve with whipped cream, a generous drizzle of golden syrup (maple or corn syrup as substitutions) and a sprinkle of cinnamon for good measure.

Ingredients:

50 g butter
½ - ¾ cup caster sugar
4 jumbo - XL eggs
500 ml buttermilk
15 ml vanilla essence
60 ml flour
1 pinch of salt
250 ml fresh cream (whipped)

Method:

Preheat oven to 160° C.

Combine the butter and sugar in a bowl. Beat until fluffy.

Separate the eggs and add the yolks one at a time, beating well after each addition.

Fold in the buttermilk.

Beat the egg whites until soft peaks form.

Fold in the softly whipped fresh cream.

Grease a baking dish (rectangular).

Pour in the batter. Bake until a golden brown.

Dust with powdered cinnamon.

Serve with more sweetened whipped cream and golden syrup.

Green Tea Ice Cream

Ingredients:

1½ cups water
¾ cup sugar
2 tbsp. loose Chinese gun-
powder green tea or green tea
(about 3 tea bags)
4 tsps. fresh lemon juice
1¼ cups whole milk

Method:

1. Combine water and sugar in a small saucepan; bring to a boil, stirring until sugar dissolves. Add tea; cover and steep 5 minutes. Strain tea mixture through a fine sieve into a bowl; discard tea leaves. Stir in lemon juice; chill completely.

2. Stir in milk. Pour mixture into the freezer can of an ice-cream freezer; freeze according to manufacturer's instructions. Spoon the ice cream into a freezer-safe container; cover and freeze 2 hours or until firm.

Say ye: "We believe in Allah, and the revelation given to us, and to Abraham, Ismail, Isaac, Jacob, and the Tribes, and that given to Moses and Jesus, and that given to (all) prophets from their Lord: We make no difference between one and another of them: And we submit to Allah (in Islam)." (2:136)

From "Growing Up Before Islam"

—Nancy E. Biddle—

About the one and only time my parents ever went to Church each year was at Christmas. We were not a religious family and it was more or less a festive way to celebrate more than paying homage to the meaning behind the season. To my recollection it only happened a few times, and then they just left off going. However, one of the times we went was particularly memorable.

As usual, my mom had the meal all planned out to eat at six, she put the turkey in the oven and we all went out to Church. It was within walking distance, about 20 minutes away and there had been just a light snow the night before so it was a beautiful festive walk. On the way home we became aware of the glorious smell of roasting turkey and as we drew nearer to our house we realized it was coming from our kitchen. Normally it takes 6 hours to roast a 15 lb turkey but it smelled done in just an hour and a half!

My mom rushed into the kitchen to find she had put the oven on self-clean in her rush to leave the house. Everyone pitched in to prepare the vegetables and we sat down for our dinner at two pm. The bird was crisp on the outside but juicy and tender on the inside. We never used that method again for cooking a turkey in less time, but if you are ever in a rush, I recommend it! Of course, we never let Mom forget it. Every season we reminisce.

Kala Jamoon—India/Pakistan

Ingredients:

350 gms. khoya
200 gms. paneer
65 gms. plain flour (1/8 cup)
600 gms. sugar
4 cups water
½ tsp. cardamom powder
1 tbsp. milk if required
ghee for deep frying

Method:

Make 1 string syrup of sugar and water.

Mash, grate or crumble khoya and paneer together.

Add cardamom powder, flour and knead well till smooth. If too dry, add a little milk.

Form a soft dough.

Make small balls out of dough rolling lightly between palms. The balls should be half the size of ping pong balls.

Heat ghee till slightly fuming. Cool for 3 minutes.

Add some balls, and allow them to rise before putting back on heat.

Fry on low heat, till dark from all over.

Drain and dip into syrup. Allow to soak till next batch is ready.

Repeat till all dough is exhausted. Drain and transfer to serving dish.

NOTE: Take care not to fry on high or the jamoons will stay undone from the center. If the jamoons are cracking, add some more milk. If soaking too much fat, add a little more flour. A little variation is necessary since the khoya may not be uniform each time.

Peach Cobbler Dump Cake—USA

Ingredients:

1 (18.5-ounce) package yellow cake mix
2 (16-ounce) cans peaches in heavy syrup
½ cup butter
½ tsp. ground cinnamon, or to taste

Method:

Preheat oven to 375° F (190° C).

Empty peaches into the bottom of one 9 x 13 inch pan.

Cover with the dry cake mix and press down firmly.

Cut butter or margarine into small pieces and place on top of cake mix.

Sprinkle top with cinnamon.

Bake at 375° F (190° C) for 45 minutes.

The Prophet said, "If somebody eats something forgetfully while he is fasting, then he should complete his fast, for Allah has made him eat and drink." (Hadith by Bukhari, Volume 8, Book 78, Number 662).

Black Forest Bread—USA

Ingredients:

1¾ cups all-purpose flour
½ cup unsweetened cocoa
1 tsp. baking soda
½ tsp. salt
½ cup dried cranberries
1 tbsp. hot water
2 tsps. instant coffee granules
¾ cup low-fat buttermilk
2/3 cup sugar
1/3 cup honey
2 tbsp. vegetable oil
2 tsps. vanilla extract
1 large egg
Cooking spray

Method:

Preheat oven to 350° F.

Combine first 4 ingredients in a large bowl.

Stir in cranberries; make a well in center of mixture.

Combine water and coffee granules; add buttermilk, sugar, honey, oil, vanilla, and egg, stirring well with a whisk.

Add to flour mixture, stirring just until moist.

Spoon batter into an 8 x 4-inch loaf pan coated with cooking spray.

Bake at 350° F for 50 minutes or until a wooden pick inserted in center comes out clean.

Cool 10 minutes in pan on a wire rack, and remove from pan.

Cool completely on wire rack.

Saira's Chocolate Filled Thumbprint Cookies—USA

Ingredients:

1 cup butter
1 cup brown sugar
2 tsp. vanilla
3 cup flour
½ cup chocolate chips
(Mini chips are best)
2 Tbsp. milk
½ tsp. salt
½ cup powdered sugar

Method:

1. Cream together the butter and brown sugar. Stir in the milk and vanilla.

2. Add the flour and salt, then the chocolate chips. It will be a very stiff dough.

3. Form into balls that are about the size of walnuts. Place on an ungreased cookie sheet about 2" apart.

4. Press your thumb into each ball of dough. This will make the depression that will hold the filling.

5. Bake at 350° F for 15 minutes, or until light golden brown. Remove from baking sheet, cool slightly and roll in powdered sugar, OR use a sieve and dust the cookies with powdered sugar—less messy!

6. When cool, put a generous ½ tsp. of chocolate filling (below) in each cookie.

Chocolate Filling Ingredients:
1¾ cup chocolate chips
2 Tbsp. shortening (Crisco)
¼ cup corn syrup
2 Tbsp. water
1 tsp. vanilla

Method:

1. In the microwave in a glass, microwave safe, 4 cup measuring bowl, melt together the chocolate chips, shortening, and corn syrup. Heat for 1 minute at a time, and stir occasionally, watching carefully that it does not boil over.
2. Stir in the water and vanilla so that all is well combined. Cool for 5 minutes, then fill

cookies. It helps to chill the cookies in the fridge to set the filling, before you put them away. Once the filling has chilled and set, it will not melt at room temperature.

Makes about 3 dozen. It is not a typo: this cookie contains no baking powder or soda, and no eggs.

Besbousa—Egypt

Ingredients:

4 heaping tbsp. of Crisco or butter
1¼ cup of sugar
1 carton of plain or vanilla yogurt (I use low fat vanilla when in the US and regular in Egypt)
1 cup milk—any kind, skim to full cream—I have used them all and it doesn't affect the taste so I use skim. Got to cut calories where you can, right?
Pinch of baking soda
Coconut
Nuts
2 cups semolina flour;
2 tbsp. melted butter

SUGAR SYRUP:
2 cups of sugar, 1½ cups of water, either vanilla or almond flavoring (depends on what you like and the nuts you use) and lemon juice—about half of one lemon. Boil all this together on top of the stove while besbousa is in the oven.

NOTE: Gets better the next day; I keep mine in the refrigerator.

Method:

Cream sugar and Crisco together, add yogurt, baking soda, flour and mix; add milk and mix.

Let stand in warm spot for about an hour if you like fluffy besbousa. Get a cookie sheet that has a rim or other type of shallow pan and grease it.

Sprinkle a little besbousa flour over the greased sheet. Add dough and spread evenly across pan. Sprinkle coconut across top of besbousa as thinly or thickly as you like.

Add nuts, if desired. Drizzle melted butter across the top and put in oven at 350° F for about ½ an hour or until the top is golden brown.

Make sugar syrup and spoon over hot besbousa: You spoon ½ of the syrup over the besbousa, let it absorb (about 5 minutes) and spoon the rest over it.

Cut into sections as decoratively as you like and serve.

Pumpkin Bread Pudding—USA

Ingredients:

1 lb. firm French bread
2 cups Half and Half (half milk, half cream)
1½ cups sugar
3 eggs
15-ounce pumpkin pie mix (seasoned)
½ cup raisins
½ cup pecans
whipped cream

Method:

Lightly grease a medium casserole dish.

Pre-heat the oven to 350° F.

Tear the bread into medium pieces and add to a mixing bowl.

Sprinkle on the sugar.

In a separate bowl, lightly beat the eggs.

Add the half and half and pumpkin mix.

Toss the mixture with the bread. Place half in the casserole.

Add the raisins and pecans.

Top with the other half of the mixture.

Bake for 25-35 minutes or until firm and lightly brown.

Serve warm with whipped cream

Saira's Brownies to Die For—USA

Ingredients:

1 cup flour
¼ tsp. baking soda
¼ tsp. salt
5 tbsp. butter
¾ cup sugar
2 tbsp. of water or cold coffee
1-6 or 8 oz. package chocolate chips. (Use real chocolate chips—not the imitation flavored)
1 tsp. vanilla extract
2 eggs
½ cup chopped walnuts (optional)

Method:

1. Preheat oven to 325° F.

2. Grease an 8 or 9 inch square pan.

3. In a medium saucepan, combine the butter, sugar and other liquids. Bring just to a boil. Remove pan from heat.

4. Add the bag of chocolate chips to the butter/sugar mixture and stir until the chips melt.

5. Add the eggs, one at a time and beat after each addition.

6. Gradually blend in the flour, soda and salt. Add the nuts if you're using them. Spread the mixture in the prepared pan.

7. Bake 30-35 minutes—do not over bake.

Cool completely before cutting. Makes an 8 x 9 or 9 x 9 inch pan full.

Specialties

Bean Dip—Mexican

This dip is surely a "must have" for holiday parties! It's also so easy that once your friends or family taste it they will be fighting over who will bring it to the next party!

Ingredients:

2 10-oz. cans refried beans
1 small container sour cream (8 oz.)
1 package shredded lettuce
1 16-oz. jar chunky salsa
2 small cans green chilies
1 tomato (diced)
2 tsp. dried cilantro
2 cups finely shredded cheddar and jack cheese
large oven-safe platter or dish

Method:

1. Spread both cans of refried beans evenly around the platter leaving approximately 1 - 2 inches around the edge for garnishing.

2. Spread approximately ½ of the container of sour cream over the layer of beans.

3. Spread the salsa on top of that layer.

4. Then, layer the shredded lettuce.

5. Finally, cover the entire top with the shredded cheese.

6. Garnish around the rim and center with the green chilies and diced tomato (you can also add black olives).

7. Sprinkle with cilantro and heat in a 350° F oven until cheese is melted and dish is heated through (can also be served cold).

8. Serve with tortilla chips and enjoy!

Creamy Yogurt-and-Walnut Dip—Turkey

This is a rich, Turkish delight for raw vegetables, pitas or meat. You'll need 12 hours prep time for the yogurt.

Ingredients:

2 cups plain low-fat yogurt
2 garlic cloves, minced
¼ cup finely chopped walnuts
1/8 tsp. salt
1/8 tsp. pepper
dash of hot sauce
2 (6-inch) pitas, each cut into 8 wedges

Method:

Place a colander in a 2-quart glass measuring bowl or medium bowl.

Line colander with 4 layers of cheesecloth, allowing cheese-cloth to extend over outside edges of bowl.

Spoon yogurt into colander, and cover loosely with plastic wrap; refrigerate yogurt 12 hours. Spoon yogurt cheese into bowl, and discard liquid.

Stir in minced garlic, chopped walnuts, salt, pepper, and hot sauce, and let mixture stand 15 minutes. Serve dip with pita wedges.

The Prophet Muhammad (peace be upon him) said: "Feed the hungry, visit the sick and set free the cap-tives." (Sahih Al-Bukhari, Volume 7, Hadith 552.)

Humpty Dumpty Had a Great Roll

—Juli Herman—

Whenever there were any hard boiled eggs that needed peeling, I could count on three pairs of little helping hands, eager to reveal the soft shiny flesh of a food item they love so much. On my cue, they would gently roll the eggs back and forth on the table, applying gentle pressure until skeins of cracks appeared on their eggs. Then peeling would take place, and you could see the joy lighting up their faces in the process.

One day, I proceeded to do some baking, and duly employed those little hands to aid me, much to their elation. However, only one of them appeared in response to my call while the other two dallied upstairs. As I bustled across the kitchen, setting up cake pans, preheating the oven and taking out the ingredients, I gave my five-year-old the heads up to crack the eggs which I had put out earlier in small bowls on the table.

"Okay, you can crack the eggs now, Hamzah."

With my back toward him, I worked at the sink, trusting him to carry out his job appropriately. He didn't utter a word as he worked, and in my occupation with what I was doing, I didn't turn around to see if he was doing all right. I assumed he knew what to do.

Soon after, two more pairs of hands arrived, ready to work with the eggs. I still kept my back to them, trusting my eight-year-old to crack the rest of the eggs in the bowl, as I had taught her.

"Ummi! Hamzah broke the egg and it's all spilled on the table and floor!"

On the table lay a broken egg, the white running down the edge of the table onto the floor while the yolk sat still, a proud proof of the remnants of Hamzah's handiwork. He had apparently 'cracked' the egg the only way he knew how, and it began to dawn on me that I hadn't actually taught him how to crack an egg.

Saira's Chorizo (Mexican Sausage)

Ingredients:

1 lb regular ground turkey,
NOT ground turkey breast—
some fat is necessary for the
best flavor.
2 cloves garlic, crushed
1 tbsp. chili powder
1 tbsp. white vinegar
1 tsp. dried oregano

Method:

Mix all the ingredients in a
medium mixing bowl.

Let sit for several hours or
overnight before using so
flavors can blend.

QUANTITY: Makes 1 lb.

NOTE: ¼ cup of this recipe equals 1 chorizo sausage in a recipe. The
sausage will keep well for several days in the refrigerator, but transfer
it to a glass or pottery bowl or jar. You'll never get the smell of it out
of plastic! Try it instead of ground beef in chili. Delicious!!

The Prophet also quoted God as saying: "O son of
Adam, I asked you for food and you fed Me not." God
was then asked: "O Lord, how should I feed You when
You are the Lord of the worlds?" In reply, God said:
"Did you not know that My (servant) asked you for
food and you fed him not? Did you not know that had
you fed him, you would surely have found (the reward
for doing so) with Me?" (Hadith Qudsi 18)

Saira's Homemade Turkey Sausage—USA

Ingredients:

1½ lbs. ground turkey
(NOT breast only; some fat
is required for best flavor.)
2 tsp. salt
1 tsp. freshly ground black
pepper
2 tbsp. brown sugar
2 tsp. ground sage
¼ tsp. nutmeg
½ tsp. ground or leaf thyme
½ tsp. red pepper flakes
(optional—for very spicy
sausage)
½ tsp. toasted fennel seed
(optional—for an Italian style
sausage)

Method:

Mix all the ingredients
together in a medium size
bowl, lightly but thoroughly.
If you wish to taste for seasonings, cook a little beforehand. You can intensify the
herbs or spices to your taste.

Let sit 8 hours or overnight.

Form into small patties and
fry in a skillet sprayed with
cooking spray. (This sausage
is so low-fat that you'll need
to spray the skillet to keep the
patties from sticking.)

QUANTITY: Makes 1½ lbs. of
bulk sausage

Nur's Special Chicken Wings

—Honey Chicken Wings—

Ingredients:

3 lbs. chicken wings
salt—to taste
freshly-ground black
pepper—to taste
1 cup honey
½ cup soy sauce
2 tbsp. vegetable oil
2 tbsp. ketchup
½ garlic clove—minced

Method:

Cut off and discard chicken
wing tips.
Cut each wing into 2 parts
and sprinkle with salt and
pepper.
Combine remaining ingredients and mix well.
Place wings in slow cooker
and pour sauce over.
Cook 6 to 8 hours on LOW.

—Oriental Chicken Wings—

Ingredients:

3 lbs. whole chicken wings or
drumettes
1 cup soy sauce
¾ cup brown sugar
½ cup water
1 tsp. lemon juice
¼ tsp. dry mustard
¼ tsp. garlic powder
½ tsp. salt
¼ tsp. ginger

Method:

Discard the tips from the
chicken wings and cut wings
apart.
Place pieces in the crock-pot.
Combine the remaining 8
ingredients into a bowl and
mix well together.
Pour over chicken. Cover.
Cook on Low for about 6
hours or on High for about 4
hours or until chicken is
done.

—Spicy Cajun Buffalo Wings—

Ingredients:

3 or more lb. chicken wings or
small chicken legs
1 bottle Kraft Spicy BBQ
sauce or K.C. Style sauce
1½ tsp. red cayenne pepper
¼ tsp. salt
2 tsp. black pepper
½ tsp. garlic flakes, minced
1 tsp. onion flakes, minced
3 tbsp Worcestershire sauce
2 tbsp Green Dragon or
jalapenos sauce
1 tbsp Tabasco sauce
1 tbsp Cajun Spice or Capt.
Link's Cajun seasoning

Method:

In your crock pot, add
chicken, BBQ Sauce, and
all spices.
Stir occasionally.
Use a low heat for 4 hrs.

The Prophet Muhammad (peace be upon him) said:
"Being rich does not mean having a great amount of
property, but [it] is being content [with what one has]."
(Sahih Al-Bukhari, Volume 4, Hadith 453)

Saira's Maple Turkey Breakfast Sausage

Ingredients:

1 lb. ground turkey
2 tbsp. REAL maple syrup OR
3 tbsp. maple sugar
2 tsp. to 1 tbsp. ground sage,
depending on how much you
like sage
½ tsp. coarsely ground black
pepper
1½ tsp. salt

Method:

Mix all the ingredients
together and let sit overnight
for flavors to blend.

Form into small patties and
fry in a lightly greased skillet.

QUANTITY: Makes 1 lb. of
sweet, mild, low-fat sausage

NOTE: Maple Sugar is a product that is pretty hard to find outside of
the New England states, but if you happen to live in the area and
have some, that's great.

The Holy Qur'an, 107:1-3 "Have you ever considered
(the kind of person) who denies the Judgment (to
come)? Behold, it is (the one) who repulses the orphan
(with harshness) and feels no urge to feed the needy."

Mango Till We Die

—Juli Herman—

Born and raised in a tropical country, mangoes have always been one of my favorite fruits. My father is also a fruit fan, and always managed to come home on market day with crates of fruits. Whenever we paid a visit to Indonesia, we would always return back home with crates of mangoes and whatever fruits were in season then.

One time, my father bought so many mangoes that our kitchen was perfumed with the sweet ripening scent of mangoes for days. Every day, I crept downstairs stealthily, gingerly tiptoed to the kitchen and grabbed a big fat mango. Within seconds, I was peeling the mango, revealing the luscious golden flesh.

As soon as the last strip of skin was peeled off, I turned on the faucet, washed the fruit and bounded back upstairs to the book I was reading, lying face down with its spine protruding in the middle. In ultimate delight, I sat back, a ripe huge mango, unsliced and uncut in my right hand, and my book in the other.

It was the most heavenly book reading experience in my life, as the sweet flesh of yellow fruit melted away in my mouth while I devoured the words in my book. In a matter of minutes, the golden treasure in my right hand was rendered to a long piece of hard pit. As if drugged, I put my book down yet again, dashed downstairs, took another ripe mango from the crate on the kitchen counter, and began peeling. The cycle repeated itself throughout the day, without anyone noticing, except for the sharp eyes of my grandmother.

Upon seeing the crate being robbed of its overflowing volume, and my tummy being filled to a hideous expansion, she said to me, "Do you know, that I had a friend who died of eating too many mangoes?"

I was barely ten then. I believed her. Suffice it to say, the crate of mangoes was left untouched by me for quite some time after that.

Warda's Sauce Pomodoro

Serve this rich sausage-tomato pasta sauce over linguine or spaghetti.

Ingredients:

1 lb. of halal sausages
(mild or sweet)
1 tbsp Olive oil
2 tsps. garlic, minced
4 cups crushed tomatoes
(Roma tomatoes work best)
1 tbsp oregano
1/8 tsp. crushed red pepper
flakes

Method:

Split the sausage casings and coarsely crumble the meat into a heavy saucepan.

Add the olive oil and slowly brown the sausage.

Remove the cooked meat with a slotted spoon.

Save to add back to the sauce at the end of cooking or use in another recipe (like pizza).

Add the garlic and cook 3 minutes.

Add the remaining ingredients.

Reduce the heat and simmer for 1½ hours, stirring frequently.

QUANTITY: Makes about 1 quart.

Flaxseed Falafel Sandwich

Ingredients:

1/3 cup flaxseed
1 (19-ounce) can chickpeas
(garbanzo beans)
2 garlic cloves, crushed
¼ cup chopped fresh parsley
2 tbsp. fresh lemon juice
1 tsp. ground cumin
½ tsp. salt
¼ tsp. ground coriander
¼ tsp. ground red pepper
¼ cup dry breadcrumbs
1 tbsp. flaxseed
2 large egg whites,
 lightly beaten
1 tsp. olive oil
cooking spray
4 (6-inch) pitas, cut in half
8 curly leaf lettuce leaves
Mediterranean chopped salad
½ cup plain fat-free yogurt

Method:

Place 1/3 cup flaxseed in a
blender or clean coffee
grinder, and process until
ground to measure ½ cup
flaxseed meal; set flaxseed
meal aside.

Drain chickpeas over a bowl,
reserving liquid.

Place chickpeas, garlic, and
1 tbsp. reserved liquid in
blender; pulse 5 times or until
coarsely chopped.

Add flaxseed meal, parsley,
and next 5 ingredients (lemon
juice through red pepper);
pulse just until mixture is
combined.

Divide chickpea mixture into
8 equal portions, shaping each
into a ½-inch-thick patty.

Combine breadcrumbs and
1 tbsp. flaxseed in a shallow
dish.

Dip patties in egg white;
dredge in breadcrumb
mixture.

Heat the oil in a large non-stick skillet coated with cooking spray over medium-high heat.

Add patties; cook 5 minutes on each side or until browned.

Line each pita half with a lettuce leaf; fill each pita half with 1 patty and about 3 tbsp. Mediterranean Chopped Salad.

Top each with 1 tbsp. yogurt.

SERVINGS: Eight

The Holy Qur'an 6:118: So eat of (meats) on which Allah's name hath been pronounced, if ye have faith in His signs.

Black-Eyed Pea Humus—Saudi Arabia

Ingredients:

3 garlic cloves, peeled
½ cup fresh lemon juice
(about 2 lemons)
1/3 cup tahini
(sesame-seed paste)
1 tsp. ground cumin
½ tsp. salt
½ tsp. paprika
2 (15.8-ounce) cans black-eyed peas, drained
14 (6-inch) pitas, quartered
fresh chives (optional)

Method:

Drop garlic through chute of food processor with processor on; process 3 seconds or until garlic is minced.

Add lemon juice and the next 5 ingredients (tahini through peas).

Process until smooth, scraping sides of bowl occasionally.

Serve with pita wedges.

Garnish with fresh chives, if desired.

As Salaam' Alaykum and Happy Eating!

—Widad—

Definitions of Terms

Black seed: An annual herbaceous plant, nigella sativa is planted in the winter, flowers in the spring and is harvested in the early summer for its jet-black seeds.Black cumin seed, or black seed for short, is believed to be native to the Mediterranean region but has been cultivated into other parts of the world including the Arabian peninsula, northern Africa and parts of Asia.

The plant has no relationship to the culinary kitchen herbs, cumin or caraway.

Bruised ginger: In Asian cooking ginger is almost always used fresh, either minced, crushed or sliced. Fresh ginger can be kept for several weeks in the salad drawer of the refrigerator. Dried ginger should be 'bruised' by beating it to open the fibers, then infused in the cooking. Store dried and powdered ginger in airtight containers.

Castor or caster sugar: is the name of a very fine sugar in Britain, so named because the grains are small enough to fit though a sugar "caster" or sprinkler. It is sold as "superfine" sugar in the United States. Because of its fineness, it dissolves more quickly than regular white sugar, and so is especially useful in meringues and cold liquids. It is not as fine as confectioner's sugar, which has been crushed mechanically (and generally mixed with a little starch to keep it from clumping).

Chorizo: Traditionally a pork sausage originating from the Iberian peninsula and known as Chouriço in Portugal. This spiced meat is usually made from coarsely chopped fatty pork and usually seasoned with chili and paprika. The mild Spanish paprika used gives this sausage its characteristic flavor. The Chorizo itself can be found as either picante (hot) or dulce (sweet). Some varieties are hung in cold dry places to cure, as happens with jamyn serrano (ham). The Pamplona variety grinds the meat further. The recipes here substitute turkey for the pork, thus making the meat halal.

Crock Pot: A brand name for a Slow Cooker.

Garam masala
- powdered blend of spices that may include cloves, cardamom, cinnamon, black peppercorns, nutmeg, mace.
- garam means "hot", but not chili hot, hot in the sense that these spices are said to increase body temperature. Interestingly, many of these spices are used in deserts in western cooking (i.e. cloves, cinnamon, nutmeg, and mace)
- different regions use different mixtures (masalas) and proportions. Garam masala will also vary from household to household.
- powdered garam masala is often added at the end of cooking in small quantities
- whole garam masala is used in north Indian cooking, especially meat dishes.
- A whole garam masala could include whole cinnamon sticks, bay leaves, cloves, cardamom (black or green), whole mace, and black peppercorns.
- Often these are fried in hot oil before other wet ingredients such as meat, onions, garlic, and/or ginger are added. Cooking with these spices release a wonderful botanical odor that fills your house and neighborhood.

Golden syrup: long popular in Britain, is becoming more broadly available in this country. Lyle's Golden Syrup is the most common brand, and we have seen it in supermarkets in some pretty out-of-the-way places. It is also available in specialty stores and online. Golden syrup, like molasses, is a product of the process of refining sugar. It is simply sugar cane juice that has been boiled down. It has the consistency of corn syrup, but a golden color and a taste different from either light or dark corn syrup, and also substantially different from its cousin, molasses. If you must, you can try substituting it with 2 parts light corn syrup and 1 part molasses or equal parts of honey and light corn syrup.

Half and Half: A mixture of half cream, half milk. The fat content is between 10 and 12 percent.

Milk bi-products from India/Pakistan: Julie Sahni, author of *Classic Indian Cooking* (Canada, UK) and other important books, says there are no more sacred or important natural products to Indians than cow's or buffalo's milk. The milk is traditionally made into five products: yogurt (dahi), clarified butter (ghee), Indian cheese (chenna or paneer), thickened milk sauce (rabadi), and milk fudge (khoya). Milk is also drunk as a beverage, but it is served warm and sweetened with a bit of sugar or honey. In a nation with a preponderance of vegetarians, Sahni says milk and milk products account for the chief source of protein.

Mirin: is an essential condiment used in Japanese cuisine, with a slightly sweet taste. It is a kind of rice wine similar to sake, but with a lower alcohol content. In the Edo period, Mirin was drunk as a sweet sake.

Panchphoran: Panchporan is a Bengali Spice Mixture Consisting of: Whole Cumin Seeds, Whole Fennel Seeds, Whole Nigella Seeds, Whole Fenugreek Seeds, Black Mustard Seeds

Tahini: A paste of ground sesame seeds and a flavor similar to peanut butter.

Useful Websites

A dictionary of cooking terms website you may find useful is:
http://southernfood.about.com/library/info/bldictionary.htm

Another cooking site, O Chef, has some excellent cooking questions
with answers at: http://www.ochef.com/Fruit.htm

Cookbook Reviews

Halal Food, Fun, and Laughter: A Literate Cookbook
Muslim Writers Publishing
www.muslimwriterspublishing.com
ISBN: 097678615X, $12.95, 142 pp.

When I was a child I spent a great deal of time in my grandmother's kitchen, chopping onions, stirring stew, or whipping up a batch of cookies, while "Grammy" told me tales of her childhood. *Halal Food, Fun, and Laughter*, by Linda D. Delgado, recaptures the spirit of Grammy's kitchen, combining short stories and poems about cooking and food, delightful animated spoon comics, and recipes from around the world. The result is a warm, good feeling inside, coupled with delicious food on your table.

Also featured in the cookbook are quotes from the Qur'an (Islam's Scripture) and hadith (narrations from the life of Prophet Muhammad), reflecting the Muslim faith of the author and the contributing writers and poets. I can guarantee you will learn something about the Islamic faith that you will never see on the evening news. The quotes are accessible and interesting; the stories and poems range from engaging and interesting, to fun and inspiring. It's like having your Chicken Soup for the Muslim soul, and eating it too.

As a cookbook aficionado, I was surprised to find that each recipe sounded better than the previous. Usually when I am flipping through one of my cookbooks looking for a recipe, I come across concoctions that make me wonder who in their right mind would even try them, let alone relish them. The recipes in *Halal Food, Fun and Laughter* all sounded delicious. I'm looking forward to trying them all

PAMELA K. TAYLOR
MIDWEST BOOK REVIEW - JUNE 2006

～

Halal Food, Fun and Laughter is a small paperback cookbook that is only small in size, but packs a great punch. This is a 142-page cookbook that is filled with wonderful recipes, adorable cartoons like sketches, spiritual quotes, and a wonderful collection of poems and anecdotal stories from the author's family and friends. Don't be fooled by the title and not look inside. Although this is supposed to be a collection of Muslim recipes and Middle Eastern cuisine, it is so much more. I would be more inclined to call it an International Collection of recipes. The book goes from Judy's Baba Ghanou, to Oriental Chicken Wings, to Charlotte Russe, to Beef Stew to American Style Macaroni and Cheese.

The book is divided into the following sections: Introduction, Soups and Salads, Main Dishes, Side Dishes, Desserts, and Specialties. I personally was thrilled to find a recipe for the Chicken Tangine because I now have an excuse to go to Williams-Sonoma and buy a Tangine Pan.

One of the recipes that I tried and enjoyed very much was Nur's Peanut Chicken Breast. I am a great fan of the crock-pot and peanuts so this recipe was a match made in heaven. Try it for yourself and see.

This recipe was delicious and my family enjoyed it. I served it with rice, although I'll bet it would be great with couscous.

As I said, this book has many wonderful recipes. There is basically one recipe to a page and they are done in a column format, making them easy to read. My only 2 minor criticisms are: I wish the book had laid flat for ease of recipe preparation and in a few recipes there are some metric measurements. The author provides a conversion chart, but I'm lazy. I might be tempted to just do the conversions for the recipes if the book was going to be reprinted.

I would highly recommend this book. You can feel the love in the manner in which the author put this book together. You get a sense of the things that are important to her: Allah, family, friends and food.

REVIEWED BY: ELISE V. FEINER
NEW HARTFORD, NEW YORK

❧

First, please accept my thanks for choosing me to review your cookbook. It was a very interesting project and far different from other cookbooks I've read/reviewed.

I very much liked the Table of Contents rather than an Index, and the conversion table in the back of the book. This makes cooking so much easier for many readers. The fact that most recipes were complete on one page is another plus. Even though a few were longer, it was easy to follow onto the next page for only a few sentences. The recipe format was easy to read with 'ingredients' and 'method' clearly separated and the two columns not crowded on the page.

The stories, poems and personal touches really provide a window into the people who have contributed to your book as well as to you yourself for having chosen these pieces.

REVIEWED BY SANDY OLSON
NORTHWOOD, INDIANA

∿

I was one of the lucky six who received a copy of Linda Delgado's book, *Halal Food, Fun and Laughter*, to read, review and cook from. I spent a few hours enjoying this book while waiting for my Dad to come out of surgery. What a pleasant way to keep my mind occupied during my wait.

Even though the target audience for this book is Muslim cooks, I think cookbook collectors who are interested in other cultures would find this book to be an interesting addition to their collections. If you like trying new recipes from around the world, then this is a great little book.

Many of the recipes in this book were contributed by Linda's "sister friends" from around the world. Some are recognized in the book while others wished to remain anonymous.

Linda has a cute little character featured in the book called "Ms. Don't Do" spoon, which often appears in little cartoons. Also scattered occasionally among the recipes are some funny food stories and poems. My favorite is the *Sleep Cooking* poem.

Since this book is targeted to Muslims, she also includes some quotes from the Qur'an, Hadith and the 5 Pillars of Islam.

I enjoy new and different cookbooks as well as learning about new cultures, people and places, especially through the foods they eat. Even though I wasn't that knowledgeable about the Muslim faith, I enjoyed reading and learning from this book.

Most of the recipes in this book are easily found at your local supermarket. The only things you might have difficultly finding are anchoor (dried mango) powder, asafpetoda (I bought some of this at a Middle Eastern store while in CA), ghee, and preserved lemons. These ingredients are only called for in a couple of recipes and can probably be found with a little searching. Flax seed is also called for in a couple recipes and can be found at most health food stores.

REVIEWED BY JOAN OSBORNE
BOOMER, NORTH CAROLINA

I'm really late with this review (and hope I do it correctly) but not because I didn't enjoy Linda's great cookbook. My husband and I went camping, so I was saving her book to enjoy while sitting by a roaring campfire, coffee in hand and a beautiful rushing stream in front of me. Complete peace and quiet. So I settled down to luxuriate in another creative author's cookbook and I wasn't disappointed.

With all that said, I totally and completely enjoyed reading through this book. First of all, it is very different than any I own or have seen. Her family stories are rich and entertaining. I especially liked her beginning phrase, "I have never been a gourmet cook but I have always been a gourmet eater". So clever. The recipes are varied, healthy, easy to understand and follow and so tempting. I am most anxious to try her Pound Cake on page 90. I use pound cake for so many things and one being my specialty, trifle.

REVIEWED BY HAZEL J. HAYNES
IDAHO

Sometimes (not all that often, mind you) I admit to feeling a tiny bit sorry for my husband Hans when he sighs as I come home with new cookbooks. He has occasionally even been heard to say something along the lines of "but you already have so many, how could you need more"? This from a man who has been collecting postage stamps since he was seven years old and regularly buys bulk sale lots to add to his collection! Even Hans somewhat unwillingly admits that I was correct in my estimate that we probably have over 750,000 stamps in the house. Almost 200,000 of these form his 'proper' collection, which is beautifully displayed in large albums.

Holland is a tiny country with a relatively large population and there just simply isn't enough space for everyone to have a big house, so many of us live in tiny "dolls' houses." To put this into perspective a bit, the respective population densities per square kilometre of Australia, Canada, United States and Holland are 2, 3, 30 and 395. Unfortunately, my capacity for cookbook book acquisition is still based on the habits I acquired in Australia where a couple, or even a couple of boxes, of new cookbooks barely made a dent in the available storage space. Not so here, I'm afraid to say.

I was proudly showing Hans a recent new addition to my cookbook collection when he said rather enthusiastically "Oh good…" I thought, ever so briefly, that I had hit the jackpot until he finished the sentence with "…it's quite small!" Some people will just never understand us, will they?

Well, that's (more than) enough idle chatter. Let's get on with the task at hand. My new cookbook, with its 'minimum storage space seal of approval' is the subject of this review.

For the third time in as many weeks I have the pleasure of reviewing a book written by one of the members of our group. (CookbooksEtCetera) As you may remember, early this month Linda Delgado asked for people who would be willing to help her with reviewing her new cookbook. I'm pleased to say that I was among the lucky people to have been given the opportunity to take part in the project and I have thoroughly enjoyed the experience. My cookbook collection covers a wide range of topics but I have 5 main themes, one of which is ethnic cookbooks. Linda's book contains Halal recipes and I have to admit that, prior to reading the book, I knew little about this topic—thank goodness for Wikipedia! Linda has told me that the edited edition of the book will include a short explanation about Halal food and cooking—I am sure that will be a very welcome addition for many readers.

The book, *Halal Food, Fun and Laughter,* is a delightful collection of recipes gathered by Linda from many different people. Throughout the book there are Hadith (sayings related to the prophet Muhammed) and Qur'an quotes (from the holy book of Islam), most of which are related in some way to food. I have to admit that I spent quite some time in "Google mode" as I was almost embarrassed by my ignorance of the Islam faith and Halal. The book also includes humorous but often thought provoking poems and short stories as well as many delightful cartoons based on a wooden spoon with a chef's hat and a wonderful sense of humour! As you can see, this charming little book offers far, far more to the reader than just recipes. My preference is for cookbooks with that 'something extra' and this book certainly qualifies.

Linda told me that she collected the recipes from different sources over several years and she has now sadly lost contact with some of the contributors. The style of the book reflects the diversity of the contributors as Linda has left the recipes in the same form in which they were given to her. This adds to the book's charm and emphasises the personal nature of the collection. It is like being able to take a peek into different kitchens in many countries and 'meet' with the cooks themselves.

The forerunner of the present book was a true labour of love from Linda. She used to put recipe cards into the pockets of small photo albums and added Arabic graphics and personalised front pages. Linda sold these mini artworks at local bazaars and fêtes but, unfortunately, the cost of the coloured inks used for the decoration meant that the books were extremely expensive to produce. Although Linda didn't mention this, I imagine that they were also incredibly time consuming to make. Fortunately, for those of us not lucky enough to own one of these original editions, Linda decided to publish her collection in book form. It is this book which I am now lucky enough to have to add to my collection.

I have never before been involved with the 'birth of a cookbook' and I have been delighted to be involved with Linda's project, even in such a small way. It has been an exciting and rewarding experience. It will be very interesting to see the edited version when it becomes available in the future so I can compare the two versions of the book. Perhaps I will even be able to recognise some of my ideas in the finished product. I am beginning to realise the amazing amount of work that the author of a cookbook has to do before a book hits the shelves and I salute all cookbook authors—especially those amongst our own ranks. Well done, all of you.

I had told Linda that I didn't know how soon I would be able to complete my proofreading/review. I actually completed the task in less than 24 hours as I found the book almost 'un-putdownable'.

If you are looking for a charming addition to your own collection or a delightful gift for the "cookbook collector with (nearly) everything" this book would be a great choice.

REVIEWED BY MARIE RIEUWERS
NETHERLANDS

∼

NOTE: The cookbook reviewers belong to a well-organized cookbook collectors group known as CookbooksEtCetera. Members are serious collectors with members having hundreds of cookbooks in their personal collections. Some members are authors of cookbooks; some write columns for Food Sections of newspapers. All love cookbooks and love to review and share their knowledge. I count myself fortunate to have happened upon this group in cyberspace and to have been accepted as a member of CookbooksEtCetera.

LINDA D. DELGADO
AUTHOR/PUBLISHER OF *Halal Food, Fun and Laughter*

About the Author

Linda D. Delgado, known by many as Widad, is a Muslim revert, the mother of three and grandmother of eight. She is a graduate of the University of Phoenix and retired as a Sergeant in 2000 from the Arizona Department of Public Safety.

Mrs. Delgado is the author of the award winning Islamic Rose Books series, which you can read about at:
    www.widad-lld.com

and *A Muslim's Guide to Publishing and Marketing*, which you can read about at:
    www.MuslimWritersPublishing.com

Islamic Rose products can be found by going to the Islamic Rose Store at:
    http://www.cafepress.com/islamicrose/

Widad's reversion story can be read at:
    http://www.IslamOnline.net

She is the founder of Islamic Writers Alliance at:
    http://www.islamicwritersalliance.net

Printed in the United States
77140LV00008B/46-51

9 780976 786153